MW00885730

BONAIRE

TRAVEL GUIDE

2024-2025

Discover the Top Attractions, Pristine Beaches, Dive Sites, Local Cuisine, Cultural Experiences and Everything You Need to Make Your Caribbean Escape Unforgettable.

Gina T. Watson

Copyright © 2024 by Gina T. Watson

All rights reserved. No part of this book may be reproduced, distributed, or transmitted in any form or by any means, including photocopying, recording, or other electronic or mechanical methods, without the prior written permission of the publisher, except in the case of brief quotations embodied in critical reviews and specific other noncommercial uses permitted by copyright law

TABLE OF CONTENTS

INTRODUCTION..8

    About Bonaire...11

    Why you should Visit Bonaire.................................13

    Quick Facts about Bonaire.....................................16

    History and Cultural Overview...............................18

CHAPTER 1..20

PLANNING YOUR TRIP...20

    Best Time to Visit... 23

    Duration of your trip..25

    Bonaire on a budget...27

    Choosing the right tour package.......................... 30

    Entry Requirements... 33

CHAPTER 2..35

GETTING TO BONAIRE...35

    Choosing the Best Flights...................................... 36

    Bonaire airport: Arrival and Orientation............38

    Flights to Bonaire... 40

    Arriving by Cruise Ship..42

    Getting Around in Bonaire.....................................44

    Bus Options...44

CHAPTER 3..47

ACCOMMODATION OPTIONS....................................... 47

    Hotels and Resorts...50

    Guesthouses and B&Bs.. 54

    Vacation Rentals... 56

    Camping Options.. 59

CHAPTER 4..62

TOP ATTRACTIONS... **62**

Washington Slagbaai National Park...............................63

Klein Bonaire..65

Bonaire National Marine Park..................................... 68

Donkey Sanctuary Bonaire... 70

CHAPTER 5...**72**

OUTDOOR ACTIVITIES...**72**

Snorkeling and Diving Spots.. 72

Windsurfing and Kitesurfing... 75

Hiking and Biking Trails..78

Bird Watching and Flamingo Spotting in Bonaire.............80

CHAPTER 6...**83**

BEACHES AND WATERSPORT.....................................**83**

Best Beaches... 85

Beach Safety Tips.. 86

Kayaking and Paddleboarding..................................... 88

Fishing and Boating... 89

CHAPTER 7...**91**

CULTURAL EXPERIENCES.. **91**

Local Festivals and Events in Bonaire........................... 93

Museums and Historical Sites......................................95

Art Galleries and Local Crafts..................................... 97

CHAPTER 8...**99**

DINING AND NIGHTLIFE... **99**

Top Restaurants.. 101

Local Cuisine and Must-Try Dishes.............................102

Bars and Nightlife Spots...104

Food Markets and Street Food.................................... 106

CHAPTER 9...**108**

SHOPPING..**108**

    Best Shopping Areas.. 109

    Souvenirs to Buy..111

    Local Markets.. 113

CHAPTER 1o..**115**

Day Trips and Excursions.. **115**

    Exploring Nearby Islands...115

    Boat Tours... 117

    Adventure Tours.. 120

    Itineraries.. 123

CHAPTER 10..**128**

PRACTICAL INFORMATION AND RESOURCES..............**128**

    Currency and Banks..131

    Language and Communication..................................... 133

    Emergency Contacts... 135

    Health and Safety Tips.. 138

    Useful Apps, Websites and Map for Your Bonaire Trip.. 141

CONCLUSION...**144**

INTRODUCTION

Bonaire, a small island in the Caribbean, is a hidden gem waiting to be discovered. Known for its stunning coral reefs, crystal-clear waters, and vibrant marine life, Bonaire offers a unique blend of natural beauty and tranquil charm. The island is a paradise for divers and nature lovers, with its pristine beaches, rich wildlife, and welcoming local culture. Unlike many other Caribbean destinations, Bonaire remains unspoiled and authentic, providing a perfect escape from the hustle and bustle of everyday life.

My journey to this island paradise began with a serendipitous encounter—a photograph of Bonaire's flamingo-filled salt flats under the golden glow of a setting sun. That image ignited a curiosity that led me to embark on an adventure unlike any other.

When I arrived on Bonaire for the first time, I was struck by the island's vibrant colors and warm, welcoming atmosphere. The air was filled with the scent of the sea, and the laid-back pace of life instantly put me at ease. My adventure began in Kralendijk, the island's main town, where the pastel-colored buildings and friendly locals made me feel right at home. As I wandered through the streets, I quickly realized that Bonaire was unlike any other destination I had visited.

One of the most memorable experiences was my first snorkeling trip at a popular spot called "1000 Steps," a beautiful beach renowned for its underwater wonders.

I descended a limestone staircase into crystal-clear waters and discovered a vibrant ecosystem teeming with life—colorful coral reefs, playful sea turtles, and the elusive dance of seahorses. The diving was incredible, like being in an aquarium. Bright fish swam around colorful coral, and sea turtles moved slowly by, unbothered by people. Each day, I explored new snorkeling sites, each offering its own unique beauty and marine life.

Another highlight was kayaking through the mangrove forests of Lac Bay. Paddling through the serene waterways, I was immersed in nature's tranquility. The mangroves formed a lush, green canopy overhead, and the only sounds were the gentle splash of my paddle and the chirping of birds. It was a peaceful escape from the hustle and bustle of daily life, and I felt a deep connection with the natural world around me.

The experience that truly stood out was encountering the flamingos at Gotomeer. Seeing these elegant birds in their natural habitat was a sight to behold. Their bright pink feathers contrasted beautifully with the blue water, creating a picture-perfect scene. I spent hours watching them wade gracefully through the shallow lake, feeling a sense of awe and wonder at their beauty. This was a moment of pure magic that I will never forget.

Bonaire offers more than just underwater beauty. Washington Slagbaai National Park, with its cactus forests and volcanic rocks, presents a wild landscape different from the beaches. Hiking there felt like discovering a hidden world.The warmth and hospitality of the locals made my stay even more special. I often found myself chatting with residents, learning about their way of life and discovering hidden spots that only they knew about.

As I reflect on my time in Bonaire, I am filled with gratitude for the experiences and memories I made. The island's unspoiled beauty, rich marine life, and genuine hospitality left a lasting impression on me. Each day was a new adventure, filled with discoveries and moments of awe.

In this travel guide, you'll find everything you need to plan your perfect Bonaire vacation. From the best diving spots and outdoor adventures to local cuisine and cultural experiences, this book covers it all. You'll get insider tips on where to stay, what to eat, and how to make the most of your time on the island. Whether you're an experienced traveler or visiting Bonaire for the first time, this guide will help you uncover the island's hidden gems and create unforgettable memories.

About Bonaire

Situated in the Leeward Antilles of the southern Caribbean Sea, Bonaire stands out as a captivating destination renowned for its pristine landscapes and inviting island charm. As a special municipality of the Netherlands, Bonaire combines Dutch influence with a distinct Caribbean allure, offering visitors a unique blend of cultural richness and natural splendor.

Bonaire, along with its sister islands Aruba and Curaçao, forms the ABC islands, situated approximately 80 kilometers (50 miles) off the coast of Venezuela. What sets Bonaire apart is its arid climate, a rarity among Caribbean islands, which ensures warm, sunny weather throughout the year. More significantly, Bonaire lies outside the hurricane belt, providing a stable climate ideal for year-round outdoor activities and exploration.

The island's ecological wealth is safeguarded by the Bonaire National Marine Park, overseen by Stichting Nationale Parken Bonaire (STINAPA). This protected area encompasses not only the pristine reefs and sandy beaches of Bonaire but also the neighboring islet of Klein Bonaire. Divers and snorkelers flock to Bonaire for its exceptional underwater diversity, boasting some of the healthiest coral reefs globally and an abundance of marine life. From vibrant fish species to majestic sea turtles and even shipwrecks steeped in history, Bonaire's marine ecosystems offer a paradise for underwater enthusiasts.

Historically, Bonaire was part of the Netherlands Antilles until its dissolution in 2010, after which it became a special municipality within the Kingdom of the Netherlands, alongside Sint Eustatius and Saba. This affiliation has fostered a strong Dutch influence evident in the island's governance and cultural practices. The population of Bonaire, predominantly Dutch nationals, reflects a blend of heritage from the former Netherlands Antilles and Aruba, contributing to the island's multicultural fabric.

The etymology of "Bonaire" traces back to the Caquetio indigenous language, with "Bonay" meaning "low country." This name reflects the island's flat, coastal terrain, which early Spanish and Dutch explorers adapted to "Bojnaj" and eventually "Bonaire." Despite the misconceived translation of "good air," the name actually refers to the geographical features that characterize this tranquil Caribbean haven.

In conclusion, Bonaire beckons travelers with its untouched beauty, warm hospitality, and a wealth of natural wonders waiting to be explored. Whether you're drawn to its world-class diving, serene beaches, or rich cultural heritage, Bonaire promises an unforgettable escape into the heart of the Caribbean.

Why you should Visit Bonaire

Bonaire is a hidden gem in the Caribbean, offering a perfect mix of adventure, relaxation, and natural beauty. If you're looking for a destination that's not crowded with tourists and has plenty of unique experiences to offer, Bonaire is the place for you. Here are some reasons why you should visit Bonaire.

First, Bonaire is a paradise for anyone who loves the water. The island is famous for its incredible diving and snorkeling spots. The water is crystal clear, and the coral reefs are full of colorful fish and other marine life. Whether you are an experienced diver or trying it for the first time, Bonaire has something for everyone. The Bonaire National Marine Park protects the reefs, ensuring they remain beautiful and healthy.

Bonaire is also great for other water activities. You can go windsurfing, kiteboarding, kayaking, or paddleboarding. The steady trade winds and calm waters make it an ideal place to try these sports. Even if you're a beginner, there are plenty of schools and instructors to help you get started.

The island's natural beauty extends beyond the water. Washington Slagbaai National Park is a must-visit. It's a large nature reserve with stunning landscapes, including cactus forests, rugged cliffs, and beautiful beaches. You can hike, bike, or drive through the park, enjoying the wildlife and breathtaking views. Keep an eye out for the island's famous flamingos, which can often be seen in the park's salt flats.

Bonaire's laid-back atmosphere is another big draw. The island is much quieter and less developed than many other Caribbean destinations. There are no high-rise hotels or large resorts. Instead, you'll find charming bungalows, small guesthouses, and local cafes. This makes Bonaire a perfect place to unwind and escape the hustle and bustle of everyday life.

The local culture in Bonaire is warm and welcoming. The people are friendly and proud of their island. You'll find that many locals are happy to share their favorite spots and tips with you. There are also local festivals and events where you can experience the island's culture and traditions.

Food is another reason to visit Bonaire. The island's cuisine is a delicious mix of Caribbean flavors and fresh seafood. You can enjoy dishes like grilled fish, conch stew, and shrimp at local restaurants. There are also many international restaurants if you're in the mood for something different. Don't forget to try some of the local fruits and sweets.

Bonaire is also committed to sustainability. The island has many eco-friendly practices and initiatives to protect its natural environment. This means you can enjoy your vacation knowing that you are supporting a destination that cares about its future.

Bonaire is a place where you can truly relax. Whether you're lounging on a quiet beach, exploring the underwater world, or enjoying a meal with a view, the island's peaceful vibe helps you unwind and recharge.

Bonaire is an amazing destination for anyone looking for adventure, natural beauty, and relaxation. Its clear waters, vibrant coral reefs, and welcoming atmosphere make it a perfect escape from the everyday. So, pack your bags and get ready to discover why Bonaire should be your next travel destination. You won't be disappointed.

Quick Facts about Bonaire

Location: Bonaire is a small island in the southern Caribbean Sea, part of the Dutch Caribbean.

Capital: Kralendijk is the capital city, located on the western coast.

Language: Dutch and Papiamento are official languages; English and Spanish are widely spoken.

Currency: The US Dollar (USD) is the official currency.

Time Zone: Bonaire operates on Atlantic Standard Time (AST), UTC-4.

Population: Approximately 20,000 residents, known as "Bonairians."

Climate: Tropical climate with warm temperatures year-round. Dry season from January to September, rainy season from October to December.

National Parks: Bonaire boasts two main parks: Washington Slagbaai National Park and Bonaire National Marine Park.

Coral Reefs: Renowned for pristine coral reefs and excellent diving opportunities.

Flamingos: The island hosts a significant population of Caribbean flamingos.

Transportation: Rental cars, scooters, and bicycles are common; taxis are available but it's best to arrange in advance.

Electricity: Standard voltage is 127V; North American-style flat two-pin plugs are used.

Health and Safety: Low crime rates; modern medical facilities available; travel insurance recommended.

Local Culture: Rich cultural heritage influenced by African, European, and Caribbean traditions.

Eco-Friendly Destination: Bonaire prioritizes sustainable tourism practices and environmental conservation.

These facts provide a snapshot of what makes Bonaire a unique and appealing destination in the Caribbean.

History and Cultural Overview

Bonaire has a rich history that blends influences from indigenous peoples, European colonization, and African heritage. Before European arrival, the island was inhabited by the Caiquetio people, who were part of the Arawak tribe. They lived off the land and sea, leaving behind cave paintings and artifacts that reflect their culture.

In 1499, the Spanish explorer Alonso de Ojeda was the first European to discover Bonaire. Over the next centuries, the island changed hands several times between the Spanish, Dutch, and British due to its strategic location and valuable salt production.

By the early 17th century, the Dutch established control over Bonaire, along with nearby Aruba and Curaçao, forming what became known as the Dutch Caribbean islands. The Dutch West India Company developed salt production on Bonaire, which became a vital export and economic activity that continues today.

The African influence on Bonaire's culture is significant due to the transatlantic slave trade. Enslaved Africans brought to work on plantations and in salt pans contributed to the island's diverse cultural heritage. Their traditions, music, and language merged with indigenous and European influences, creating a unique cultural tapestry that defines Bonaire today.

In 1954, Bonaire became part of the Netherlands Antilles, a federation of Dutch Caribbean islands. In 2010, the island gained special municipality status within the Kingdom of the Netherlands, alongside Aruba and Curaçao, after the dissolution of the Netherlands Antilles.

Today, Bonaire embraces its multicultural identity. The local culture is celebrated through music, dance, cuisine, and festivals. Traditional events like the Simadan harvest festival and Dia di Rincon showcase Bonairean heritage and offer visitors a chance to experience local customs and flavors.

The island's cultural attractions include museums, art galleries, and historical sites that highlight its past and present. Visitors can explore historic buildings in Kralendijk, the capital city, or visit the Bonaire Museum to learn more about the island's history and natural environment.

Bonaireans are known for their warm hospitality and pride in their island. They welcome visitors to experience their way of life, from enjoying local dishes like goat stew and keshi yena (stuffed cheese) to participating in traditional dances and music performances. Exploring Bonaire's history and cultural diversity adds depth to any visit, offering insights into the island's evolution and the resilience of its people.

CHAPTER 1.

PLANNING YOUR TRIP

Before embarking on your journey to Bonaire, it's essential to lay the groundwork for a smooth and memorable experience. Planning your trip involves careful consideration of various factors to ensure everything from transportation and accommodation to activities and logistics align seamlessly.

Start by envisioning your ideal Bonaire vacation. Are you drawn to the island's renowned diving spots, eager to explore its rich marine life? Perhaps you're seeking tranquil beaches where you can unwind and soak up the Caribbean sun. Or maybe it's the rugged landscapes of Washington Slagbaai National Park that pique your interest. Whatever your preferences, Bonaire offers a diverse range of attractions and activities to suit every traveler.

Next, consider the practical aspects of your trip. Research the best time to visit based on weather patterns and seasonal activities. Bonaire enjoys a tropical climate year-round, with dry, sunny days dominating most of the year. Understanding the climate and its implications on your travel plans will help you pack appropriately and make the most of your stay.

Transportation is another crucial consideration. Whether you're arriving by air or sea, familiarize yourself with the available options for getting to Bonaire. Flights from major hubs in the United States, Europe, and nearby Caribbean islands serve Bonaire's Flamingo International Airport. Alternatively, cruise ships frequent Bonaire's port, offering a different perspective for travelers arriving by sea.

Accommodation choices on Bonaire range from luxurious resorts to intimate guesthouses and vacation rentals. Depending on your budget and preferences, you can opt for beachfront villas with stunning ocean views or cozy cottages nestled amidst the island's serene landscapes. Booking accommodations in advance ensures you secure your ideal retreat, whether you prefer proximity to diving sites, bustling town centers, or secluded beach fronts.

Activities and excursions play a central role in shaping your Bonaire adventure. Dive enthusiasts can explore the island's world-class reefs, while nature lovers can hike through the rugged terrain of the national parks. Cultural experiences abound, from sampling local cuisine to attending traditional festivals and exploring historical landmarks. Planning ahead allows you to prioritize activities that align with your interests and make the most of your time on the island.

Familiarize yourself with practical considerations such as local customs, currency, and health information. Bonaire operates on the US Dollar, and English is widely spoken alongside Dutch and Papiamento. Understanding cultural norms and etiquette ensures respectful interactions with locals, enhancing your overall experience.

By meticulously planning your trip to Bonaire, you set the stage for a fulfilling and unforgettable journey. This chapter provides essential guidance to help you navigate the nuances of travel preparation, ensuring your visit to this Caribbean gem exceeds expectations and leaves you with cherished memories for years to come.

Best Time to Visit

Choosing the best time to visit Bonaire depends on your preferences and what you want to do during your trip. Bonaire enjoys a warm, tropical climate year-round, making it a pleasant destination almost any time of the year. However, there are some factors to consider to make the most of your visit.

The dry season, from January to September, is generally considered the best time to visit Bonaire. During these months, the weather is sunny and dry, with low chances of rain. This makes it ideal for outdoor activities such as diving, snorkeling, hiking, and exploring the island's natural attractions like Washington Slagbaai National Park.

If you're specifically interested in diving and snorkeling, the months of April to June and September to October are recommended. These periods offer excellent visibility underwater, with calm seas and comfortable water temperatures. You'll have a good chance to see vibrant coral reefs and a variety of marine life during these months.

The summer months from July to August are the hottest and can be a bit more humid, but they still offer plenty of opportunities to enjoy Bonaire's beaches and outdoor activities. Keep in mind that this is also the peak tourist season, so popular attractions and accommodations may be busier.

The rainy season, from October to December, typically sees more frequent showers and increased humidity. While Bonaire doesn't experience hurricanes like other Caribbean islands, occasional showers can occur. However, these months are also quieter in terms of tourism, offering a more laid-back atmosphere and sometimes better deals on accommodations.

The best time to visit Bonaire depends on your preferences for weather, activities, and crowd levels. Whether you prefer the dry season for optimal outdoor adventures or the quieter rainy season for a more relaxed experience, Bonaire welcomes visitors year-round with its warm hospitality and natural beauty.

Duration of your trip

Deciding how long to stay in Bonaire depends on what you want to experience and your travel preferences. Whether you're planning a short getaway or a longer vacation, here are some factors to consider when determining the duration of your trip.

Consider the activities you want to do. If you're primarily interested in diving or snorkeling, you might want to stay longer to explore different dive sites and reefs. If you prefer relaxing on the beach or exploring the island's cultural attractions, a shorter stay might suffice.

Think about your travel pace. A shorter trip can be perfect for a quick escape or focused exploration of specific attractions. On the other hand, a longer stay allows for a more relaxed schedule, giving you time to unwind and fully immerse yourself in the island's charm.

Depending on the time of year you visit, you may want to adjust the duration of your trip. During the dry season (January to September), you might prefer a longer stay to take advantage of optimal weather and outdoor activities. In the rainy season (October to December), a shorter trip might be sufficient if you're concerned about occasional showers.

Consider travel logistics such as flight schedules and availability. If you're traveling a long distance to reach Bonaire, you might want to stay longer to make the most of your journey. Conversely, if you have limited vacation time, a shorter trip can still provide a fulfilling experience.

Your budget can also influence the duration of your trip. A longer stay may require more funds for accommodations, meals, and activities. However, Bonaire offers options for different budgets, from luxury resorts to budget-friendly guesthouses, allowing you to tailor your trip duration accordingly.

The duration of your trip should align with your personal preferences and goals. Whether you're planning a weekend getaway, a week-long vacation, or an extended stay, Bonaire offers something for every traveler.

Consider these factors when planning your trip to Bonaire to ensure you have a rewarding and enjoyable experience exploring this Caribbean paradise.

Bonaire on a budget

Visiting Bonaire without overspending is entirely feasible with some savvy planning and smart choices. Here's how to experience this Caribbean island on a budget:

Accommodations: Opt for budget-friendly options like guesthouses, hostels, or vacation rentals, which often provide comfortable stays at lower costs than larger hotels. Booking in advance can help secure better rates.

Eating Out: Explore local eateries, food trucks, and smaller restaurants where you can enjoy delicious meals at reasonable prices. Sampling Bonairean specialties such as fish stew and fresh seafood allows you to savor local flavors without breaking the bank.

Self-Catering: Choose accommodations with kitchen facilities to prepare your own meals using ingredients from local markets or grocery stores. This approach is often cheaper than dining out for every meal and offers flexibility in meal times.

Transportation: Consider renting a car, scooter, or bicycle for exploring the island independently. Public transportation options are limited, but taxis and shared van services can be used for shorter trips if needed. Planning your transportation needs ahead can help minimize costs.

Free and Low-Cost Activities: Take advantage of Bonaire's natural attractions for free or low-cost activities. Snorkeling from public beaches, hiking in national parks like Washington Slagbaai, and exploring local markets and historical sites are all affordable ways to enjoy the island.

Water Activities: Diving and snorkeling are popular in Bonaire. Bringing your own equipment can save on rental fees, and many snorkeling spots are accessible from shore, reducing the need for costly boat trips.

Seasonal Deals: Look for seasonal promotions and discounts on accommodations, tours, and activities. Traveling during off-peak times, such as the rainy season or shoulder seasons, often means lower rates and fewer crowds.

Local Culture: Immerse yourself in Bonaire's culture through free or low-cost activities such as attending cultural festivals, visiting art galleries, or exploring historic sites. These experiences provide insights into the island's heritage without straining your budget.

Water and Sun Protection: Bring reusable water bottles and sunscreen to avoid high costs at tourist shops. Staying hydrated and protected from the sun ensures you remain comfortable throughout your trip without unnecessary expenses.

By planning ahead, choosing affordable accommodations and activities, and embracing local culture, you can enjoy Bonaire on a budget while still experiencing the island's natural beauty and unique charm. Adjust your plans based on personal preferences and enjoy a memorable and affordable adventure in Bonaire.

Choosing the right tour package

When planning your trip to Bonaire, selecting the right tour package can significantly enhance your experience on the island. Here are some tips for choosing the perfect tour package:

Identify Your Interests: Consider what interests you most about Bonaire. Are you looking forward to diving and snorkeling adventures, exploring cultural heritage sites, or experiencing nature reserves? Knowing your preferences will help you find a tour package that aligns with your interests.

Check Itinerary and Activities: Review the itinerary and activities included in the tour package. Make sure it offers a mix of activities that you are eager to participate in. Look for packages that include key attractions or experiences you want to enjoy during your trip.

Duration and Flexibility: Consider how long the tour package lasts and whether it fits your schedule. Some packages are designed for specific durations with fixed itineraries, while others may offer more flexibility in terms of activities and duration. Choose a package that allows you to explore Bonaire at your preferred pace.

Inclusions and Exclusions: Pay attention to what is covered in the tour package, such as accommodations, meals, transportation, and entrance fees to attractions. Be clear about any items that are not included or any additional costs that may arise to avoid surprises during your trip.

Reviews and Recommendations: Research reviews and recommendations from other travelers who have taken the tour package. Their feedback can provide valuable insights into the quality of the tour, the expertise of guides, and overall satisfaction with the experience.

Budget Considerations: Determine your budget for the tour package and compare different options within your price range. While cost is important, consider the value and experiences offered by each package to make an informed decision that aligns with your budget and expectations.

Local Expertise: Choose tour operators or agencies with local expertise and knowledge of Bonaire. Experienced guides can enhance your experience by sharing insights into local culture, history, and wildlife, making your tour more informative and enjoyable.

Customization Options: Some tour packages may offer customization options to tailor the experience to your preferences. Whether it involves adding extra activities, adjusting the itinerary, or upgrading accommodations, inquire about customization possibilities to personalize your trip.

By considering these factors, you can select a tour package that matches your interests, budget, and travel style, ensuring a memorable and fulfilling experience exploring Bonaire. Whether you seek adventure, relaxation, or cultural immersion, the right tour package will help you make the most of your visit to this captivating Caribbean destination.

Entry Requirements

Before traveling to Bonaire, it's important to know the entry requirements to ensure a smooth arrival and enjoyable stay. Here's what you need to consider:

Passport: You must have a valid passport to enter Bonaire. Ensure your passport is valid for at least six months beyond your intended stay to avoid any issues.

Visa: Citizens of many countries, including the United States, Canada, European Union countries, and others, do not need a visa for short visits to Bonaire (typically up to 90 days). However, visa requirements can vary based on your nationality, so check with the nearest consulate or embassy of Bonaire for specific visa requirements.

Tourist Card: Some travelers may need to obtain a tourist card upon arrival in Bonaire, depending on their nationality. This card allows you entry and typically needs to be purchased upon arrival at the airport. Check if you need a tourist card before traveling.

Customs Regulations: Be aware of customs regulations when entering Bonaire. This includes restrictions on bringing certain items such as firearms, drugs, and large quantities of alcohol or tobacco. Familiarize yourself with these regulations to avoid any delays or issues at customs.

Travel Insurance: While not a formal entry requirement, having travel insurance is highly recommended. It can provide financial protection in case of unexpected events during your trip, including medical emergencies, trip cancellations, or lost baggage.

By understanding and fulfilling these entry requirements before your trip, you can ensure a hassle-free arrival and start enjoying your time exploring Bonaire without any concerns. Always check for any updates or changes to entry requirements closer to your travel date to stay informed and prepared.

CHAPTER 2.

GETTING TO BONAIRE

Traveling to Bonaire is the gateway to discovering a Caribbean paradise renowned for its pristine reefs, vibrant marine life, and laid-back atmosphere. Situated in the southern Caribbean, Bonaire is a part of the Dutch Caribbean and offers a unique blend of natural beauty and cultural charm. This chapter serves as your guide to navigating the journey to Bonaire, providing comprehensive details on transportation options, flight connections, travel tips, and everything you need to know to ensure a smooth and enjoyable arrival on this captivating island.

Whether you're planning your first visit or returning to explore more of what Bonaire has to offer, understanding the logistics of getting here is essential for starting your adventure on the right foot. From international flights to local transportation tips, this chapter equips you with the knowledge to plan your journey effectively, maximize your travel experience, and begin immersing yourself in the wonders of Bonaire from the moment you arrive.

Choosing the Best Flights

When planning your trip to Bonaire, it's important to select flights that suit your preferences and needs. Here's how to find the most suitable flights for your journey:

Consider Direct vs. Connecting Flights: Decide whether you prefer direct flights or are open to connecting flights. Direct flights can be more convenient and save time, while connecting flights may offer more flexibility in terms of schedule and cost.

Flight Duration: Look at the total travel time, including layovers for connecting flights. Choose flights that minimize overall travel time and maximize your time on the ground in Bonaire.

Research Airlines: Explore different airlines that fly to Bonaire. Compare factors such as onboard amenities, baggage policies, customer reviews, and overall reputation to find an airline that meets your preferences.

Check Departure and Arrival Times: Verify departure and arrival times to ensure they align with your schedule. Consider how flight times impact your plans upon arrival in Bonaire, including accommodation check-in times.

Compare Prices: Compare prices across various airlines and booking platforms. Booking in advance can often secure lower fares, especially during peak travel seasons.

Flexible Booking Options: Look for airlines that offer flexible booking policies, such as free cancellations or changes. This provides flexibility in case your travel plans need adjustment.

Consider Airport Transfers: Plan ahead for transportation from Flamingo International Airport to your accommodation in Bonaire. Research options to ensure a smooth transfer upon arrival.

Travel Insurance: Consider purchasing travel insurance that covers flight cancellations, delays, or interruptions. This can provide financial protection and assistance in unforeseen circumstances.

By considering these factors and planning ahead, you can choose flights that align with your preferences and enhance your overall travel experience to Bonaire. Whether you prioritize convenience, cost-effectiveness, or specific airline amenities, selecting the best flights ensures a smooth start to your Caribbean adventure.

Bonaire airport: Arrival and Orientation

Arriving at Flamingo International Airport in Bonaire marks the beginning of your island adventure. Here's what you can expect upon arrival:

Airport Facilities: Flamingo International Airport is a small and efficient airport, making navigating through customs and baggage claim relatively quick and straightforward. The airport offers basic amenities such as restrooms, ATMs, and car rental services.

Immigration and Customs: Upon arrival, proceed through immigration where your passport will be checked. Visitors from many countries are granted entry for tourist purposes without needing a visa, but it's essential to check specific requirements based on your nationality before traveling. After immigration, collect your baggage and proceed through customs, where officers may ask about any items you are bringing into Bonaire.

Transportation Options: From the airport, transportation to your accommodations is readily available. Taxis are conveniently located outside the terminal, and car rentals can be arranged in advance or upon arrival. It's advisable to confirm transportation arrangements before your trip to ensure a smooth transfer.

Orientation: Bonaire is a small island, and most accommodations are within a short drive from the airport. The main town, Kralendijk, is about a 10-minute drive from the airport and serves as the hub for dining, shopping, and exploring local culture.

Local Tips: Exchange currency at the airport if needed, although US dollars are widely accepted on the island. Remember to stay hydrated and protect yourself from the sun with sunscreen and a hat, especially upon arrival in Bonaire's warm climate.

Flamingo International Airport offers a welcoming entry point to Bonaire, providing essential services and a relaxed atmosphere to start your Caribbean getaway smoothly. Enjoy your time exploring the island's natural beauty, vibrant marine life, and rich cultural heritage from the moment you arrive.

Flights to Bonaire

Getting to Bonaire by air is straightforward, with several options available depending on your location. Here's what you need to know about flights to Bonaire:

International Connections: Flamingo International Airport (BON) is the main airport serving Bonaire. It connects to various international destinations, primarily in North America and Europe. Direct flights are available from cities like Miami, Atlanta, Houston, Amsterdam, and Toronto, among others.

Major Airlines: Several major airlines operate flights to Bonaire, including American Airlines, Delta Air Lines, United Airlines, KLM Royal Dutch Airlines, and TUI Netherlands. These airlines offer regular scheduled flights to and from the island, providing convenient options for travelers.

Connecting Flights: If direct flights are not available from your departure city, connecting flights through hubs such as Miami, Atlanta, or Amsterdam can be a viable option. Connecting flights allow you to reach Bonaire with a layover in another city, providing flexibility in travel schedules.

Flight Duration: The duration of flights to Bonaire varies depending on your departure city and whether you have a direct or connecting flight. Direct flights from major US cities typically range from 3 to 5 hours, while flights from European cities may take longer due to the distance.

Booking Tips: To find the best flights, compare prices and schedules across different airlines and booking platforms. Booking in advance often results in better deals, especially during peak travel seasons. Consider flexibility in travel dates to find more affordable options.

Airport Arrival: Upon arrival at Flamingo International Airport, follow signs for immigration, baggage claim, and customs. The airport is relatively small and efficient, making it easy to navigate. Taxis and car rentals are available for transportation to your accommodations.

Travel Documentation: Ensure you have a valid passport and any required visas or tourist cards for entry into Bonaire. Check specific entry requirements based on your nationality before traveling.

Flying to Bonaire offers a convenient and efficient way to reach this Caribbean gem. Whether you prefer direct flights or connecting options, planning ahead ensures a smooth journey and allows you to start enjoying the natural beauty and laid-back atmosphere of Bonaire upon arrival.

Arriving by Cruise Ship

Arriving in Bonaire by cruise ship is an exciting way to explore this Caribbean island. Here's what you need to know about arriving by cruise ship:

Port of Kralendijk: Cruise ships dock at the Port of Kralendijk, Bonaire's main port located near the capital city. The port offers stunning views of turquoise waters and is within walking distance of shops, restaurants, and local attractions.

Shore Excursions: Cruise lines offer a variety of shore excursions to explore Bonaire's highlights. Popular activities include snorkeling or diving in pristine reefs, visiting Washington Slagbaai National Park for hiking and wildlife viewing, or exploring the historic sites of Kralendijk.

Customs and Immigration: Upon arrival at the port, cruise passengers go through a customs and immigration process similar to that at airports. Ensure you have your passport and any necessary documents ready for inspection.

Local Transportation: Transportation options from the port include taxis, rental cars, and guided tours. Taxis are readily available near the port entrance, offering convenient transportation to beaches, attractions, and shopping areas.

Shopping and Dining: The port area features local shops selling souvenirs, handicrafts, and jewelry, perfect for picking up mementos of your visit. Nearby restaurants and cafes offer a taste of Bonaire's cuisine, including fresh seafood and local specialties.

Safety and Security: Bonaire is known for its safety and hospitality towards visitors. The local tourism infrastructure ensures a pleasant and secure experience for cruise passengers exploring the island.

Local Tips: Exchange currency if needed, although US dollars are widely accepted. Take precautions against the sun with sunscreen and hats, especially during outdoor activities.

Arriving in Bonaire by cruise ship provides a convenient way to experience the island's natural beauty and vibrant culture. Whether you prefer exploring on your own or joining organized tours, Bonaire offers a memorable Caribbean experience from the moment you step ashore.

Getting Around in Bonaire.

Bus Options

Bonaire is a relatively small island, making it easy to get from one end to the other in a short amount of time. Whether you prefer the freedom of driving yourself, the simplicity of taking public transportation, or the adventure of exploring by bike or on foot, Bonaire has something to suit every traveler's style and budget.

Public Buses: Bonaire has a limited public bus service that mainly serves local residents. The buses are small vans that operate on fixed routes between Kralendijk, the island's capital, and other key areas. These buses are an affordable option, but they may not run frequently and can be less reliable for tourists looking to explore the island in depth.

Private Shuttles: Many hotels and resorts offer private shuttle services for their guests. These shuttles can provide transportation to and from the airport, as well as to popular tourist destinations around the island. Check with your accommodation to see if they offer this service and if there are any additional costs involved.

Tour Buses: For tourists, organized tour buses are a convenient way to see the island's attractions. These tours often include stops at major sights like Washington Slagbaai National Park, the Salt Pans, and the Donkey

Sanctuary. Joining a tour can be a great way to learn more about Bonaire's history and culture while ensuring you don't miss any highlights.

Renting a Car: Given the limited bus options, many visitors find that renting a car is the best way to explore Bonaire. Car rentals provide the flexibility to visit various attractions at your own pace, and the island's roads are generally well-maintained and easy to navigate.

Taxis: Taxis are also available and can be a convenient option for getting around the island, especially if you prefer not to drive. Taxis can be hired for specific trips or for the entire day, giving you the flexibility to explore without worrying about navigation.

Bicycles: Cycling is a popular and eco-friendly way to explore Bonaire. The island's flat terrain and scenic routes make it ideal for bike rides. Many hotels and rental shops offer bicycles for hire, allowing you to discover the island at your own pace. Biking is perfect for reaching beaches, nature reserves, and even local eateries while enjoying the fresh air and beautiful views.

Scooters and Motorbikes: For a bit more speed and convenience, renting a scooter or motorbike is a great option. These are available from various rental agencies on the island and can be a fun way to navigate through

Bonaire's roads. Scooters and motorbikes are especially handy for short trips and quick explorations.

Walking: Bonaire's compact size makes it easy to explore certain areas on foot. Strolling through Kralendijk, the island's charming capital, lets you experience local shops, restaurants, and historic sites up close. Walking is also a great way to explore coastal areas and take in the stunning ocean views.

Water Taxis: Given Bonaire's emphasis on marine activities, water taxis provide a unique travel option. These taxis can take you to various dive sites, snorkeling spots, and Klein Bonaire, a small, uninhabited island just off the coast. Water taxis offer a scenic and enjoyable way to reach locations that might be less accessible by land.

Combining these travel options can enhance your experience, allowing you to see different sides of Bonaire while making the most of your time on the island. Whether you prefer the independence of cycling, the adventure of kayaking, or the convenience of organized tours, Bonaire offers a variety of ways to explore its stunning landscapes and vibrant culture.

CHAPTER 3.

ACCOMMODATION OPTIONS

Finding the perfect place to stay is crucial for making your trip to Bonaire unforgettable. The island offers a wide range of accommodation options to suit every traveler's needs and preferences, from luxurious resorts to cozy guesthouses. Whether you're looking for a beachfront villa, an all-inclusive resort, or a budget-friendly hostel, Bonaire has something for everyone.

One of the first things to consider when choosing your accommodation is the location. Bonaire's main town, Kralendijk, is a popular choice for many visitors. Staying in Kralendijk means you'll be close to restaurants, shops, and nightlife, as well as the main port if you're arriving by cruise ship. If you prefer a more tranquil setting, there are plenty of options outside the town center, offering peace and quiet, often right on the beach.

For those who seek luxury, Bonaire has a number of high-end resorts and hotels that provide top-notch amenities, stunning views, and exceptional service. These establishments often feature private beaches, on-site dining, spas, and a variety of water sports activities. Many of these resorts are designed with divers in mind, offering dive packages and easy access to some of the island's best dive sites.

If you're traveling on a budget, don't worry—Bonaire has plenty of affordable options too. Budget-friendly accommodations range from charming guesthouses and B&Bs to hostels and budget hotels. These places often provide a more personal touch, with friendly hosts who can offer insider tips on the best spots to visit on the island. Staying at a budget accommodation doesn't mean sacrificing comfort, as many of these options are clean, comfortable, and conveniently located.

Vacation rentals are another popular option, particularly for families or groups. Renting a house or apartment gives you the flexibility to cook your own meals and enjoy a home-away-from-home experience. Many vacation rentals come equipped with full kitchens, multiple bedrooms, and outdoor spaces such as patios or gardens. This can be a cost-effective way to enjoy an extended stay on the island.

For those who love nature and adventure, there are eco-lodges and campgrounds available. These accommodations offer a unique opportunity to stay close to nature, often in beautiful, secluded locations. Eco-lodges are designed to have minimal environmental impact and often use sustainable practices, making them an excellent choice for eco-conscious travelers.

Choosing the right accommodation can significantly enhance your Bonaire experience. Whether you're seeking luxury, comfort, budget-friendly options, or something more adventurous, the island's diverse range of accommodations ensures that every traveler can find the perfect place to stay. Take the time to consider what's most important to you—be it proximity to diving spots, budget constraints, or a tranquil setting—and you're sure to find an option that meets your needs and helps make your Bonaire trip truly memorable.

Hotels and Resorts

Staying in one of Bonaire's diverse hotels or resorts ensures a memorable experience tailored to different preferences and budgets. Here are five great options to consider, each with its unique charm and amenities:

1. Delfins Beach Resort Bonaire: Located at 44 Punt Vierkant, Kralendijk, offers a luxurious beachfront experience. Getting there from the airport is easy; it's just a short 10-minute drive. This resort boasts spacious, modern rooms with stunning ocean views. The highlight is the swimming pool with a sandy beach, perfect for lounging. Dining at the on-site Brass Boer restaurant is a must, offering a fusion of local and international cuisines. For a day of adventure, you can snorkel right off the beach or join a diving excursion arranged by the resort.

2. Central Hotel Bonaire: Located at 20 Kaya L. D. Gerharts, Kralendijk. Bonaire is a convenient option for those who love being close to the action. It's a quick 5-minute drive from the airport. This boutique hotel offers comfortable rooms with modern amenities and a friendly atmosphere. Staying here, you're within walking distance of various restaurants, shops, and the local market. Enjoy a leisurely breakfast at the hotel before exploring Kralendijk's charming streets. For budget

travelers, this hotel offers good value with its central location and affordable rates.

3. Ocean Breeze Bonaire Apartments: Situated at 90 Kaya International, Kralendijk, these apartments are just a 3-minute drive from the airport, making your arrival stress-free. Ocean Breeze offers a range of well-furnished apartments, each with a private balcony or terrace overlooking the marina. The self-catering facilities are perfect for those who prefer to cook their meals. Spend your days exploring nearby dive sites or relaxing by the pool. The serene environment is ideal for couples and families seeking a quiet retreat.

4. The Lodge Bonaire B&B: Located at 12 Kaya Inglatera, Kralendijk, this charming bed and breakfast is a 7-minute drive from the airport. The Lodge Bonaire offers cozy, individually decorated rooms and a warm, welcoming atmosphere. Breakfast is served in a lovely garden setting, providing a perfect start to your day. The hosts are incredibly helpful, offering great local tips. You can rent a bike nearby to explore the island on a budget, or simply enjoy the peaceful surroundings of the B&B.

5. Eden Beach Resort: Located at Bulevard Gobernador Nicolaas Debrot 73, Bonaire, Kralendijk, 73 Kaya Gobernador N Debrot, Kralendijk, this resort is a 10-minute drive from the airport. Eden Beach Resort is famous for its lively beach bar, Spice Beach Club, where

you can enjoy cocktails while watching the sunset. The resort offers a range of rooms and apartments, catering to different group sizes and budgets. Spend your days diving, snorkeling, or relaxing by the pool. The beach is just steps away, offering easy access to water activities. For a more budget-friendly stay, consider their garden-view rooms which are more affordable yet still offer access to all the resort's amenities.

Travel Tips for Budget Travelers:
- Book accommodations well in advance to secure the best rates.
- Consider staying in central locations like Kralendijk to save on transportation costs.
- Choose self-catering apartments to prepare your meals and save on dining out.
- Look for hotels or B&Bs that offer complimentary breakfast.
- Take advantage of free activities such as beach outings, hiking, and exploring local markets.

Each of these accommodations offers unique experiences, ensuring that whether you're looking for luxury, convenience, or budget-friendly options, Bonaire has something that will make your stay unforgettable. From luxurious resorts to charming B&Bs, you can find the perfect place to enjoy the island's beauty and hospitality.

Guesthouses and B&Bs

Bonaire offers a variety of guesthouses and B&Bs that provide a more intimate and personal experience, often at a lower cost compared to larger hotels and resorts. Here are four excellent options, each with its own unique charm and amenities:

1. BnBBonaire - Bed and Breakfast & Apartments Near the Ocean: Located at Kaya Zepher 2, Kralendijk, Bonaire, Caribisch Nederland, Bonaire, Nederlands Antillen, Kralendijk, this B&B is just a 5-minute drive from the airport. BnBBonaire offers both rooms and apartments, making it a versatile choice for different types of travelers. The property is close to the ocean, allowing for easy access to snorkeling and diving sites. The rooms are clean, comfortable, and equipped with modern amenities. Start your day with a delicious breakfast on the terrace while enjoying the sea breeze. The friendly hosts are always available to provide local tips and recommendations. For budget travelers, the apartments with kitchenettes allow you to prepare your own meals, saving on dining costs.

2. Casa Mantana Bonaire - Boutique Guesthouse: Situated at 10a Kaya Finlandia, Kralendijk, this boutique guesthouse is about a 10-minute drive from the airport. Casa Mantana offers a cozy and stylish atmosphere with beautifully decorated rooms that reflect the island's

vibrant culture. The lush garden and inviting pool area create a tranquil retreat. Guests can enjoy a hearty breakfast each morning and relax in the communal lounge. The guesthouse is within walking distance to several restaurants and shops. Renting a bike or scooter is a great way to explore the nearby attractions without spending much on transportation.

3. B&B Kas ChuChubi - Bed and Breakfast Bonaire:
Located at 8b Kaya Finlandia, Kralendijk, B&B Kas ChuChubi is around 8 minutes by car from the airport. This charming B&B features tastefully decorated rooms with a homely feel. The hosts go out of their way to make you feel welcome, offering a warm and personalized service. Enjoy a continental breakfast in the courtyard, surrounded by tropical plants. The B&B's location in a quiet residential area ensures a peaceful stay, yet it's still close enough to Kralendijk's amenities. For those on a budget, Kas ChuChubi provides excellent value with its comfortable accommodations and complimentary breakfast.

4. Oasis Guesthouse Bonaire: Located at 17 Kaya Scorpio, Kralendijk, Oasis Guesthouse is a 7-minute drive from the airport. This guesthouse offers spacious rooms with modern furnishings and a relaxed vibe. The outdoor pool and garden area are perfect for unwinding after a day of exploring. Guests can take advantage of the shared kitchen to prepare their meals, a great option for

budget-conscious travelers. The guesthouse provides free snorkeling equipment, allowing you to explore the nearby reefs without additional costs. The friendly owners are always ready to help with planning your activities and making your stay enjoyable.

Staying in a guesthouse or B&B in Bonaire offers a unique and personalized experience that allows you to connect with the local culture and enjoy the island's natural beauty. Each of these accommodations provides a cozy, welcoming atmosphere and various amenities to ensure a comfortable and memorable stay, catering to both luxury and budget travelers.

Vacation Rentals

Opting for a vacation rental in Bonaire can provide a home-like experience with the flexibility to tailor your stay to your own preferences. Vacation rentals are perfect for families, groups, or anyone looking for a more private and personalized accommodation. Here are three excellent options to consider:

1. Sunwise Bonaire: Located at 83 Sabal Palm, Kralendijk, Sunwise Bonaire offers a variety of vacation rentals, from cozy apartments to luxurious villas. Getting there from the airport takes about 10 minutes by car. Sunwise properties are spread across different parts of the island, providing options for various preferences,

whether you want to be close to the beach, in the heart of Kralendijk, or in a more secluded area. Each rental is well-maintained and comes with amenities such as fully equipped kitchens, private pools, and outdoor spaces. To enjoy your time, start your day with breakfast on the terrace, then explore local dive sites or take a sunset stroll along the beach. For budget travelers, sharing a larger house with friends or family can be more economical than booking multiple hotel rooms.

2. Sun Rentals Bonaire: Sun Rentals Bonaire is located in 65 Kaya Grandi, Kralendijk and is about an 8-minute drive from the airport. They offer a range of rental properties, including waterfront apartments and spacious villas. Sun Rentals focuses on providing comfortable accommodations with a personal touch. The staff is very helpful in arranging activities like diving, snorkeling, and windsurfing. Spend your mornings diving in crystal-clear waters and afternoons lounging by your private pool. For those on a budget, Sun Rentals offers affordable options without compromising on comfort, and the convenience of cooking your own meals can save on dining expenses.

3. Bonaire Oceanview Rentals: Located at Kaya Virgo 5 Kralendijk, Bonaire, these rentals are approximately 10 minutes by car from the airport. Bonaire Oceanview Rentals offer stunning oceanfront properties that cater to different group sizes and budgets. Each rental is fully

equipped with modern amenities, including kitchens, Wi-Fi, and air conditioning. Enjoy breathtaking views of the ocean from your balcony or patio. This location is ideal for diving enthusiasts, with easy access to some of the best dive sites on the island. Spend your evenings dining al fresco while watching the sunset over the Caribbean Sea. Budget-conscious travelers will appreciate the competitive rates and the option to prepare their own meals, which can significantly cut down on food costs.

Staying in a vacation rental in Bonaire offers a flexible and comfortable way to experience the island. Whether you're looking for luxury or budget-friendly options, these vacation rentals provide excellent amenities and personalized experiences that can make your stay truly special. Enjoy the freedom of having your own space, the convenience of self-catering, and the opportunity to live like a local while exploring Bonaire's beautiful landscapes and vibrant culture.

Camping Options

While Bonaire is renowned for its luxurious resorts and charming guesthouses, it also offers unique camping opportunities for those seeking a closer connection with nature. Camping in Bonaire allows you to experience the island's natural beauty more intimately and is an excellent option for budget travelers and adventure enthusiasts. Here's what you need to know about camping in Bonaire:

Washington Slagbaai National Park: Located on the northern tip of the island, Washington Slagbaai National Park is a stunning natural reserve that offers designated camping areas. The park is accessible by car, about an hour's drive from Kralendijk. Camping here provides a unique opportunity to immerse yourself in Bonaire's rugged landscapes, including cacti forests, limestone plateaus, and secluded beaches. Set up your tent and wake up to the sounds of native birds and the gentle lapping of waves. During the day, explore the park's extensive hiking trails, snorkel in pristine waters, or visit the park's viewpoints for panoramic vistas. Remember to bring all necessary camping gear, including a tent, sleeping bags, and cooking supplies, as amenities are limited.

Tips for Camping in Washington Slagbaai National Park:
- Obtain a camping permit from the park's entrance or from the Bonaire National Parks Foundation office in Kralendijk.
- Pack plenty of water, food, and supplies, as there are no stores within the park.
- Practice Leave No Trace principles to preserve the park's natural beauty.
- Be prepared for varying weather conditions and pack appropriate clothing.
- Respect local wildlife and avoid feeding or disturbing animals.

Sorobon Beach Resort: While not a traditional camping site, Sorobon Beach Resort offers a unique "glamping" experience. Located at Sorobon Beach, about 20 minutes from Kralendijk, this resort features eco-friendly tent accommodations right on the beach. These tents provide a comfortable and luxurious camping experience with amenities like beds, electricity, and access to resort facilities, including a beach bar and restaurant. Enjoy activities such as windsurfing, paddleboarding, and yoga right at your doorstep. The serene environment and stunning beach views make Sorobon Beach Resort a perfect blend of adventure and relaxation.

Tips for Glamping at Sorobon Beach Resort:
- Book your tent in advance, especially during peak tourist seasons.

- Take advantage of the resort's amenities while enjoying the outdoor camping vibe.
- Participate in the resort's organized activities for a more enriching experience.
- Relax on the private beach and enjoy the tranquil surroundings.

Camping in Bonaire offers a unique way to experience the island's natural beauty and tranquility. Whether you choose the rugged terrain of Washington Slagbaai National Park, the luxurious glamping at Sorobon Beach Resort, or the adventurous spirit of Lac Bay, camping provides a memorable and immersive way to connect with Bonaire's stunning landscapes. For budget travelers, it's also an economical way to enjoy the island while being close to nature.

CHAPTER 4.

TOP ATTRACTIONS

This chapter is a journey through the island's most captivating and diverse destinations, each offering a unique glimpse into Bonaire's natural beauty, cultural heritage, and recreational opportunities.

From the moment you step onto Bonaire's shores, you're greeted by an array of experiences that cater to every interest and preference. Whether you're drawn to the pristine beaches that fringe the turquoise waters, the vibrant marine sanctuaries that beckon divers and snorkelers, or the rugged landscapes of national parks that promise adventure, Bonaire has something to captivate every visitor.

Explore the island's natural wonders, from the expansive salt flats where flamingos paint the landscape pink, to the dramatic cliffs and cactus-studded hills of Washington Slagbaai National Park. Dive into the crystal-clear waters of Bonaire National Marine Park, a sanctuary teeming with colorful coral reefs and marine life, or wander through historic sites that tell stories of Bonaire's past, from colonial forts to quaint villages with Dutch-Caribbean architecture.

Discover the flavors of Bonaire through its local cuisine, experience the warmth of its people through cultural festivals and markets, and embark on eco-adventures that unveil hidden caves, mangrove forests, and secluded beaches. Whether you're seeking relaxation, adrenaline-pumping activities, or a deeper connection with nature and culture, Bonaire's top attractions promise an enriching and unforgettable experience.

Washington Slagbaai National Park

Washington Slagbaai National Park is a rugged and picturesque sanctuary located at the northern tip of Bonaire, offering a unique blend of natural beauty and cultural heritage. To reach the park, you'll embark on a scenic drive from the main towns, navigating through winding coastal roads and desert landscapes that showcase Bonaire's raw, untamed terrain.

As you approach the park's entrance, the air becomes thick with the scent of sea salt and desert blooms. The park is open daily, and while there is an entrance fee, it's a worthwhile investment for the rich experiences that await. Upon arrival, I was greeted by friendly park rangers who provided maps and guidance for exploring the diverse offerings of the park.

One of the park's highlights is its dramatic landscapes, characterized by volcanic peaks, rugged cliffs, and expansive vistas overlooking the Caribbean Sea. Hiking trails wind through cactus forests and past towering rock formations, offering panoramic views and opportunities for wildlife spotting. I was mesmerized by the sight of native birds like the Caribbean flamingo and yellow-shouldered parrot, which call the park home.

For those seeking adventure, the park offers excellent opportunities for snorkeling and diving along its pristine coastline. Crystal-clear waters reveal vibrant coral reefs and a kaleidoscope of marine life, including colorful fish and sea turtles gliding gracefully through the underwater gardens.

Cultural enthusiasts will appreciate the historical landmarks scattered throughout the park, such as the old plantation houses and remnants of the island's colonial past. These sites provide insight into Bonaire's history and the lives of its early inhabitants.

After a day of exploration, I found a peaceful spot to enjoy a picnic amidst the natural beauty of the park, savoring the tranquility and sense of solitude that Washington Slagbaai offers. The park's commitment to conservation is evident in its pristine condition and the respect shown by visitors for its delicate ecosystems.

Washington Slagbaai National Park is a must-visit destination for anyone exploring Bonaire. Whether you're hiking the trails, snorkeling in its azure waters, or simply absorbing its natural wonders, the park offers a profound connection to the island's heritage and natural environment. It's an experience that leaves a lasting impression, inviting you to immerse yourself fully in Bonaire's unspoiled beauty and rich biodiversity.

Klein Bonaire

Klein Bonaire, meaning "Little Bonaire," is a small uninhabited island located just off the coast of Bonaire in the southern Caribbean Sea. Accessible only by boat, Klein Bonaire offers a pristine and secluded escape from the bustling mainland.

To reach Klein Bonaire, I boarded a water taxi departing from Kralendijk, Bonaire's main town. The short boat ride provided stunning views of Bonaire's coastline and the turquoise waters that surround Klein Bonaire.

Upon arrival, I was struck by the island's untouched beauty. Klein Bonaire is a protected nature reserve, ensuring its beaches and underwater ecosystems remain pristine. There is no entrance fee to visit Klein Bonaire, but some boat operators may charge for transportation.

The island's main draw is its beaches—wide stretches of soft, powdery sand lapped by calm, crystal-clear waters. I spent hours snorkeling along the vibrant coral reefs just off the shore, marveling at the colorful fish, sea turtles, and other marine life that call this underwater paradise home.

For those who prefer lounging on the beach, Klein Bonaire offers plenty of secluded spots to relax and soak up the sun. I found shade under a swaying palm tree, enjoying the tranquility interrupted only by the gentle sound of the waves and the occasional seabird soaring overhead.

Exploring the island on foot revealed its rugged beauty, with rocky outcrops and sparse vegetation contrasting against the azure sea. Birdwatchers will appreciate the opportunity to spot nesting seabirds, including the iconic brown pelicans and elegant terns.

As the day drew to a close, I watched the sun dip below the horizon, casting a golden glow over the water—a perfect end to a day of blissful relaxation and natural beauty.

Klein Bonaire is a hidden gem that shouldn't be missed during a visit to Bonaire. Whether you're snorkeling, sunbathing, or simply immersing yourself in its unspoiled surroundings, Klein Bonaire offers a serene and rejuvenating experience in the heart of the Caribbean.

Bonaire National Marine Park

The Bonaire National Marine Park is a celebrated marine sanctuary encompassing the waters surrounding Bonaire and Klein Bonaire, renowned worldwide for its pristine coral reefs and abundant marine life. Located just off the western coast of Bonaire, accessing the park is straightforward, often done by boat from Kralendijk or via guided snorkeling and diving tours.

During my visit, I embarked on a snorkeling excursion that began with a short boat ride from Kralendijk's harbor. As we approached the park's boundaries, the water transformed into a palette of blues, hinting at the vibrant underwater world awaiting us. The park operates on a fee-based entry system, with funds supporting conservation efforts and maintaining visitor facilities.

Upon entering the park's waters, I was immediately struck by the clarity and warmth of the Caribbean Sea. Snorkeling revealed a breathtaking diversity of marine life—colorful coral formations teeming with fish of all sizes and shapes, from darting parrotfish to gracefully gliding sea turtles. The reef's health and abundance were evident, a testament to the park's status as a UNESCO World Heritage site and its strict conservation measures.

Diving deeper, I encountered shipwrecks that have become artificial reefs, offering refuge to a myriad of species. The wrecks are not only fascinating to explore but also serve as reminders of Bonaire's maritime history. Guided by knowledgeable dive instructors, I felt safe and informed throughout the underwater adventure.

Above the surface, Klein Bonaire beckoned with its pristine beaches and nesting sites for seabirds, providing a peaceful contrast to the vibrant underwater scenes. After snorkeling, I relaxed on the sandy shores, soaking in the sun and reflecting on the day's encounters with Bonaire's natural wonders.

The Bonaire National Marine Park isn't just a destination for snorkelers and divers; it's a sanctuary where visitors can connect deeply with the marine environment. Whether exploring its underwater gardens, marveling at its biodiversity, or simply enjoying its tranquil beaches, the park offers an immersive and unforgettable experience for anyone seeking to explore the Caribbean's underwater treasures.

Donkey Sanctuary Bonaire

The Donkey Sanctuary Bonaire is a heartwarming refuge located on the serene island of Bonaire, dedicated to the care and preservation of donkeys. Nestled in the countryside on Kaminda Lagun, the sanctuary is easily accessible by car from Kralendijk, Bonaire's main town. The drive offers picturesque views of the island's arid landscapes and glimpses of its native wildlife.

Upon arriving at the sanctuary, I was greeted by the sight of donkeys peacefully roaming in spacious enclosures shaded by native trees. The sanctuary operates on a donation-based entry system, making it accessible to all visitors who wish to support the welfare of these gentle creatures. The donations contribute to their care, including food, medical treatment, and shelter maintenance.

Walking through the sanctuary, I observed donkeys of all ages and colors, each with a unique personality and story. Many of them approached the fence curiously, seemingly eager for interaction and the occasional treat offered by visitors. It was a joy to learn about the sanctuary's efforts to rescue and rehabilitate donkeys from various situations, providing them with a safe haven where they can live out their lives in peace.

Guided tours are available for those interested in a deeper understanding of the donkeys' history and the sanctuary's mission. Knowledgeable staff members shared insights into the donkeys' behavior, their roles in Bonaire's history, and the ongoing conservation efforts to protect them. It was evident that the sanctuary is not just a place of refuge but also an educational center promoting awareness about animal welfare and environmental conservation.

Visitors can spend time exploring the sanctuary's grounds, enjoying serene walks amidst the tranquil surroundings. I found myself captivated by the donkeys' interactions with each other and their gentle demeanor, which reflected the caring environment provided by the sanctuary.

The Donkey Sanctuary Bonaire offers a meaningful and educational experience for visitors of all ages. Whether you're a nature enthusiast, an animal lover, or simply seeking a peaceful retreat, a visit to this sanctuary provides an opportunity to connect with Bonaire's wildlife and contribute to a worthy cause. It's a place where compassion meets conservation, leaving a lasting impression of kindness and appreciation for the island's natural heritage.

CHAPTER 5.

OUTDOOR ACTIVITIES

Bonaire beckons adventurers and nature enthusiasts alike to explore its diverse landscapes and engage in thrilling pursuits. Whether you're drawn to the vibrant coral reefs teeming with marine life, the expansive national parks boasting unique flora and fauna, or the tranquil beaches perfect for relaxation, Bonaire offers an array of outdoor experiences that promise excitement, serenity, and unforgettable moments in nature.

Snorkeling and Diving Spots

Snorkeling and diving in Bonaire are unforgettable experiences that reveal the island's vibrant underwater world. The crystal-clear waters surrounding Bonaire boast some of the Caribbean's healthiest coral reefs, making it a paradise for snorkelers and divers alike.

The "1000 Steps" Dive Site: Located on Bonaire's western shore, the "1000 Steps" dive site is renowned for its stunning coral formations and diverse marine life. Despite its name, the entrance involves a rugged descent down a limestone staircase rather than an actual thousand steps. Once submerged, divers are greeted with an abundance of marine biodiversity, including colorful parrotfish, graceful eagle rays, and occasional sightings of reef sharks. The visibility here is exceptional, often reaching up to 100 feet (30 meters), making it ideal for capturing breathtaking underwater photography.

Klein Bonaire: Just a short boat ride southwest from Kralendijk lies Klein Bonaire, a small uninhabited island surrounded by some of the Caribbean's most pristine coral reefs. Snorkelers can explore shallow reefs teeming with tropical fish and vibrant corals, while divers can venture deeper to encounter larger marine species such as barracudas and sea turtles. The calm, clear waters and minimal currents make Klein Bonaire an ideal spot for beginners and experienced underwater enthusiasts alike.

Salt Pier: Situated on Bonaire's southwest coast near Kralendijk, Salt Pier is a unique dive site where remnants of a former salt mining operation have transformed into a thriving marine habitat. Divers descend alongside the pier's massive pillars adorned with colorful corals, sponges, and sea fans. Keep an eye out for tarpons and schools of silversides that seek refuge in the shadows, along with occasional visits from green sea turtles gliding gracefully through the water. Night dives here offer a magical experience, as bioluminescent creatures add a surreal glow to the underwater landscape.

Andrea I and II: Located off the coast of Bonaire's capital, Kralendijk, Andrea I and II are popular dive sites featuring sunken vessels that have become artificial reefs.

These wrecks attract a diverse array of marine life, including angelfish, moray eels, and groupers. Divers can explore the intricate structures of these ships, now adorned with vibrant coral growth and inhabited by schools of fish. Underwater photographers will appreciate the dramatic scenery and opportunities to capture stunning images of marine life thriving in their new habitat.

Tips for Snorkelers and Divers: Before embarking on your underwater adventure in Bonaire, remember to respect local marine conservation efforts by using reef-safe sunscreen and avoiding touching or disturbing marine life. Dive operators and snorkeling tours are readily available in Kralendijk and nearby resorts, offering expert guidance, equipment rental, and educational insights into Bonaire's rich marine ecosystem.

Whether you're snorkeling among vibrant reefs or diving into deeper waters, Bonaire promises an aquatic adventure like no other. Embrace the thrill of discovering hidden treasures beneath the waves and let the wonders of this Caribbean gem captivate your senses. With every dip below the surface, you'll uncover a new chapter in Bonaire's marine wonderland, leaving you with memories to cherish long after you've returned to shore. It's an experience not to be missed during your visit to this Caribbean gem.

Windsurfing and Kitesurfing

Windsurfing and kitesurfing in Bonaire are thrilling water sports that harness the island's constant trade winds and clear waters. Lac Bay, located on the southeastern coast near Sorobon Beach, is renowned worldwide for its ideal conditions for windsurfing. Here, beginners and experienced surfers alike can glide across the water's surface, propelled by steady breezes that provide perfect stability for learning new maneuvers or refining existing skills.

Windsurfing involves standing on a board and using a sail to catch the wind, propelling you across the water. Beginners can take lessons at various windsurfing schools around Lac Bay, where shallow, calm waters provide an excellent learning environment. As you progress, you can venture farther out into the bay, feeling the exhilaration of riding the wind.

Kitesurfing, on the other hand, uses a kite and a board to glide across the water's surface. Lac Bay's consistent trade winds and expansive shallow waters make it one of the best spots in the world for kitesurfing. Beginners can also take lessons here, learning how to control the kite and master the techniques needed to navigate the waves.

Both sports offer a unique perspective of Bonaire's coastline, with views of turquoise waters and distant shores. The thrill of gliding over the waves, powered by wind and skill, is an experience that will leave you exhilarated and eager to return to the water.

Sorobon Beach: Situated along Lac Bay's tranquil shores, Sorobon Beach offers a picturesque setting for windsurfing enthusiasts. The shallow, turquoise waters and sandy bottom create an inviting playground for practicing freestyle tricks or cruising along the coastline. Sorobon Beach is also home to the annual Bonaire PWA World Cup, attracting top windsurfers from around the globe to showcase their talents against the backdrop of Bonaire's natural beauty.

Kitesurfing in Bonaire: For adrenaline seekers, kitesurfing in Bonaire provides an exhilarating experience amidst the island's stunning scenery. Atlantis Beach, located on the southwest coast near the fishing village of Rincon, offers expansive stretches of sandy beaches and consistent trade winds ideal for kitesurfing adventures. Beginners can take lessons from certified instructors, while advanced riders can challenge themselves with jumps and aerial maneuvers in the clear Caribbean skies.

Atlantis Beach: Known for its reliable wind conditions and spacious shoreline, Atlantis Beach is a favorite spot among kitesurfing enthusiasts seeking both excitement and serenity. The shallow waters and sandy bottom make launching and landing kites safe and straightforward, while the panoramic views of Bonaire's rugged coastline add to the thrill of every ride. Whether you're gliding effortlessly across the waves or catching air with high-flying jumps, Atlantis Beach promises an unforgettable kitesurfing experience.

Tips for Windsurfers and Kitesurfers

Before hitting the water, check local wind forecasts and tide conditions to ensure optimal surfing conditions. Bonaire's warm climate means you can enjoy windsurfing and kitesurfing year-round, but the best months for consistent winds are typically from December to August. Safety is key in windsurfing and kitesurfing, and instructors ensure that beginners are equipped with the necessary knowledge and safety gear. They also provide guidance on reading wind conditions and understanding the local currents, ensuring a safe and enjoyable experience for all.

Hiking and Biking Trails

Hiking and biking trails in Bonaire offer a fantastic way to explore the island's natural beauty and rugged landscapes. Whether you prefer walking through serene nature reserves or pedaling along coastal paths, Bonaire provides trails suited for all levels of outdoor enthusiasts.

Washington Slagbaai National Park: Covering nearly 20% of Bonaire's land area, Washington Slagbaai National Park is a paradise for hikers and bikers alike. Trails wind through desert landscapes adorned with towering cacti and ancient divi-divi trees, leading to hidden beaches and historic landmarks like the old slave huts that offer poignant reminders of Bonaire's past. Hike to the summit of Mount Brandaris, the island's highest point, for a sunrise or sunset experience that rewards with panoramic views stretching across the island and beyond.

Biking in Bonaire: Cycling enthusiasts will find Bonaire's flat terrain and scenic coastal roads ideal for exploring the island at a leisurely pace. The southern coast near Lac Bay offers tranquil biking routes with views of azure waters and mangrove forests, perfect for a relaxing ride. For more adventurous bikers, the routes within Washington Slagbaai National Park provide a mix of challenging climbs and thrilling descents, showcasing the island's natural beauty and diverse ecosystems.

Gotomeer Trail: For a peaceful hike or bike ride, head to Gotomeer Trail, located on Bonaire's eastern side near the salt pans. This easy trail meanders through rolling hills and offers glimpses of pink flamingos wading in shallow waters, creating a picturesque backdrop for nature enthusiasts and bird watchers alike.

During my hikes and bike rides on Bonaire, I was treated to breathtaking vistas and encounters with native wildlife. The trails often lead to secluded spots where I could relax and take in the peaceful surroundings. Along the way, I passed by towering cacti, colorful birds, and occasional glimpses of the ocean sparkling in the distance.

Whether you choose to hike or bike, it's essential to come prepared with sturdy footwear, plenty of water, and sun protection. The island's climate can be hot and dry, so staying hydrated and wearing sunscreen are important. Additionally, respecting the natural environment by staying on designated trails helps preserve Bonaire's pristine landscapes for future visitors to enjoy.

Exploring Bonaire's hiking and biking trails allows you to connect with the island's natural beauty on a deeper level. Whether you're seeking adventure or a peaceful retreat into nature, these outdoor activities offer a memorable way to experience the Caribbean's hidden gem.

Bird Watching and Flamingo Spotting in Bonaire

Bird watching in Bonaire is a delightful experience for nature enthusiasts and bird lovers alike. The island's diverse habitats provide a haven for a wide variety of bird species, making it a paradise for bird watchers.

Throughout Bonaire, you'll find wetlands, mangroves, coastal areas, and inland cactus fields that attract both resident and migratory birds. One of the best places for bird watching is the Washington Slagbaai National Park, where you can spot species such as flamingos, Caribbean parrots, and brown pelicans. The park's diverse ecosystems offer different bird watching opportunities, from spotting shorebirds along the coastline to observing songbirds in the interior.

In addition to the national park, Lac Bay and Gotomeer are excellent spots for bird watching. Lac Bay's mangroves are home to herons, egrets, and kingfishers, while Gotomeer is known for its flamingos wading in the shallow waters against a backdrop of pink salt flats.

Flamingo Watching Highlight

Flamingo watching in Bonaire is a captivating outdoor activity that offers a unique glimpse into the island's natural beauty.

The island is home to a significant population of Caribbean flamingos, making it a prime destination for birdwatching enthusiasts and nature lovers alike. Two of the best places to observe flamingos in their natural habitat are Gotomeer and Pekelmeer Flamingo Sanctuary.

Gotomeer: a saltwater lagoon located in the northwest part of Bonaire, is particularly renowned for flamingo watching. Here, early mornings and late afternoons offer ideal times to observe these elegant birds as they feed and interact in their natural habitat. The sight of flamingos wading through the shallow waters against the backdrop of the island's unique pink salt flats is truly mesmerizing.

Pekelmeer Flamingo Sanctuary: located in the southern part of the island near the salt flats, is another prime location for flamingo spotting. This protected area is one of only four breeding sites for the Caribbean flamingo in the world. The sanctuary's vast, shallow lagoons provide an ideal environment for flamingos to feed and nest. Visitors can observe large flocks of these vibrant pink birds, often numbering in the hundreds, against the backdrop of the striking white salt flats and turquoise waters.

During my bird watching excursions on Bonaire, I marveled at the vibrant colors and graceful movements of the island's birdlife. Among the most memorable moments were the serene mornings spent at Gotomeer and Pekelmeer, where I observed flocks of flamingos in their natural habitats. The tranquility of the lagoons and the beauty of the surrounding landscapes made each sighting unforgettable.

Tips for Flamingo Watching
Bring Binoculars and a Camera: For a closer view and to capture the stunning scenes, binoculars and a camera are essential. A telephoto lens is recommended for photographing these birds from a distance.

Respect Their Space: Maintain a respectful distance to avoid disturbing the flamingos. Use designated viewing areas and trails to minimize impact on their natural habitat.

Combine with Other Activities: Flamingo watching can be combined with other outdoor activities such as hiking and biking. Both Gotomeer and Pekelmeer are located in scenic areas that offer additional opportunities for exploration and adventure.

Stay Hydrated and Protected: Bring water, wear sunblock, and wear a hat to protect yourself from the sun. The open areas around the lagoons can get quite hot during the day.

CHAPTER 6.

BEACHES AND WATERSPORT

Welcome to the sun-soaked shores and azure waters of Bonaire, where the Caribbean's natural beauty takes center stage. Chapter 7 delves into the island's coastal treasures and the exhilarating world of watersports, offering a comprehensive guide to making the most of Bonaire's beach fronts and aquatic activities.

From secluded coves with powdery white sands to bustling beaches perfect for socializing, Bonaire's coastline offers a diverse array of beach experiences. Each beach has its own charm, whether you're seeking solitude for relaxation or vibrant scenes with beach bars and water sports rentals.

Watersports enthusiasts will find themselves in paradise with a plethora of activities to choose from. Bonaire's warm, clear waters are ideal for snorkeling, allowing you to discover colorful coral reefs teeming with marine life just below the surface. Diving enthusiasts can explore some of the Caribbean's best dive sites, where vibrant fish and intricate coral formations await.

For those seeking an adrenaline rush, windsurfing and kitesurfing are popular choices, thanks to the island's consistent trade winds and spacious bays. Kayaking and paddleboarding offer a more serene way to explore the coastline, while boat tours provide opportunities for deep-sea fishing or sunset cruises.

This chapter guides you through the best beaches to visit, highlighting their unique features and the activities available at each location. Whether you're lounging under a palapa with a book in hand or embarking on an underwater adventure, Bonaire's beaches and watersports promise unforgettable experiences for every traveler.

Prepare to immerse yourself in the natural splendor of Bonaire's coastline, where every beach and watersport activity invites you to unwind, explore, and create lasting memories in the Caribbean sun.

Best Beaches

Te Amo Beach, close to Kralendijk, features calm, shallow waters and soft white sand, making it perfect for families and snorkelers. The nearby vibrant coral reefs are teeming with marine life.

Sorobon Beach, located on Lac Bay's eastern shore, is renowned for windsurfing and kiteboarding due to its shallow, turquoise waters and consistent trade winds. It's ideal for both beginners and experienced water sports enthusiasts.

Pink Beach, found on the southeastern coast, gets its name from the pinkish hue of its sand, created by crushed coral particles mixed with white sand. It offers excellent snorkeling opportunities and breathtaking views of the Caribbean Sea.

1000 Steps Beach, despite its name, can be reached via a steep staircase. This secluded spot on the west coast boasts crystal-clear waters, abundant marine life, and exceptional snorkeling and diving spots.

Bachelor's Beach, south of Kralendijk, is a tranquil and serene beach favored by locals and visitors alike. Its calm waters and soft sand create an ideal setting for relaxation and snorkeling.

Each of these beaches on Bonaire promises a unique experience, whether you're seeking adventure in the water, a peaceful day on the sand, or a chance to explore the island's natural beauty. Remember to bring sunscreen, snorkeling gear, and plenty of water to fully enjoy your time at these picturesque coastal retreats.

Beach Safety Tips

When you're enjoying the beaches of Bonaire, it's important to prioritize safety to ensure a memorable and worry-free experience. First and foremost, always swim in designated areas where lifeguards are present, if possible. These professionals keep a watchful eye and are trained to respond quickly in case of emergencies, making your beach day safer and more relaxed.

Knowing your swimming abilities is crucial. Stay within areas that match your skill level to avoid any unnecessary risks. If you're not a strong swimmer, consider staying in shallow waters or wearing a life jacket for added peace of mind.

Protection from the sun is another essential aspect of beach safety. Bonaire's sun can be intense, so apply sunscreen liberally and frequently, especially after swimming. Wearing a wide-brimmed hat, UV-protective sunglasses, and lightweight, long-sleeved clothing can also shield you from harmful UV rays.

Staying hydrated is key, especially in tropical climates. Bring plenty of water to drink throughout the day to prevent dehydration. It's wise to limit alcohol consumption, as it can impair judgment and increase the risk of accidents.

Be mindful of potential hazards on the beach, such as coral reefs, rocks, and marine life. Always watch where you're walking and swimming to avoid injury. Marine creatures like jellyfish and sea urchins should be admired from a safe distance to avoid accidental contact.

If you're enjoying the beach alone, it's a good idea to let someone know your plans. Swimming with a buddy not only enhances safety but also adds to the enjoyment of your beach experience.

Respect for nature is essential. Dispose of trash responsibly and refrain from activities that could harm coral reefs or disturb wildlife. Leave shells and other natural treasures where you find them for others to appreciate.

Familiarize yourself with emergency procedures and local emergency contacts before heading to the beach. Knowing how to respond to emergencies and having a basic first aid kit on hand can make a significant difference in critical situations.

By adhering to these simple guidelines, you can relax and make the most of your time at Bonaire's stunning beaches, whether you're swimming, sunbathing, or simply soaking in the beauty of the Caribbean coastline.

Kayaking and Paddleboarding

Kayaking and paddleboarding are fantastic ways to explore Bonaire's beautiful coastline. In kayaking, you paddle a small boat called a kayak, which allows you to navigate through calm waters and get close to marine life. Paddleboarding involves standing or kneeling on a large board and using a paddle to propel yourself forward. Both activities offer a peaceful way to enjoy the turquoise waters and soak in the scenery.

You can rent kayaks and paddleboards from various water sports centers around Bonaire. Popular spots to launch include Sorobon Beach on Lac Bay and beaches near Kralendijk. These locations provide easy access to calm waters perfect for beginners and opportunities to see colorful fish and coral reefs.

When planning a kayaking or paddle boarding excursion, remember to bring sunscreen, a hat, sunglasses, and a waterproof bag for your belongings. It's also a good idea to wear a life jacket, especially if you're not a strong swimmer.

Safety is important when on the water. Check the weather conditions before heading out, avoid strong winds or rough seas, and stay aware of your surroundings, including other boats and snorkelers.

Both kayaking and paddleboarding offer a relaxing way to connect with nature and enjoy a low-impact workout. Whether you're exploring mangroves, gliding over shallow reefs, or paddling to Klein Bonaire, these activities promise memorable experiences on Bonaire's pristine waters.

Fishing and Boating

Fishing enthusiasts will find Bonaire's waters teeming with a variety of fish species. Whether you prefer shore fishing, deep-sea fishing, or fly fishing, there are plenty of opportunities to cast your line and enjoy the thrill of reeling in a catch. Local guides and charters can take you to the best fishing spots, where you might hook snapper, grouper, tarpon, or even barracuda.

Boating allows you to explore Bonaire's coastline and nearby islands like Klein Bonaire. You can rent a boat for a day of leisurely cruising, snorkeling at secluded spots, or picnicking on pristine beaches accessible only by boat. Alternatively, join a guided boat tour to learn about the island's history, marine ecology, and conservation efforts while enjoying breathtaking views of the Caribbean Sea.

You can rent fishing gear and book fishing charters in Kralendijk or at local marinas. For boating, rentals and tours are available at various water sports centers along the coast. Popular boating destinations include Lac Bay, Sorobon Beach, and the calm waters around Klein Bonaire.

Pack sunscreen, a hat, sunglasses, and appropriate clothing for sun protection. If you're fishing, bring your own gear or rent equipment locally. Don't forget snacks, drinks, and a camera to capture memorable moments on the water.

Before heading out on a fishing or boating trip, check weather conditions and sea forecasts. Wear a life jacket for safety, especially if you're not a strong swimmer. Respect local fishing regulations and marine conservation efforts. Stay aware of other boats, snorkelers, and divers in the area to ensure everyone's safety.

Fishing and boating offer relaxing ways to enjoy Bonaire's natural beauty and connect with its rich marine environment. Whether you're angling for a big catch or cruising along the coast, these activities provide unforgettable experiences for visitors of all ages.

CHAPTER 7.

CULTURAL EXPERIENCES

Immerse yourself in the vibrant culture of Bonaire through a diverse array of experiences that showcase the island's rich heritage and traditions. From exploring historical landmarks to indulging in local cuisine and participating in traditional festivals, Bonaire offers a tapestry of cultural delights waiting to be discovered.

Learn about the island's fascinating history through visits to museums, historical sites, and cultural centers that chronicle its past from indigenous settlements to colonial influences. Engage with friendly locals who are eager to share their stories and proud traditions, offering insights into Bonaire's unique identity.

Delve into Bonaire's culinary scene, where fresh seafood, local ingredients, and Dutch and Caribbean flavors converge. Savor traditional dishes like keshi yena (stuffed cheese), grilled fish, and hearty stews prepared with love and passed down through generations. Don't miss the chance to dine at local eateries and food markets, where every meal is a celebration of Bonairean hospitality.

Experience the island's vibrant festivals and events that showcase its cultural vitality. From lively music festivals and traditional dance performances to religious celebrations and carnivals, each event offers a glimpse into Bonaire's spirit and community bonds. Participate in local traditions, join in the festivities, and feel the rhythm of the island's heartbeat.

Explore Bonaire's arts and crafts scene, where talented artisans create handmade treasures inspired by the island's natural beauty and cultural heritage. Browse local markets and galleries for unique souvenirs such as colorful paintings, intricately woven baskets, and handmade jewelry that reflect Bonaire's artistic soul.

Engage in cultural workshops and activities that offer hands-on experiences in traditional crafts, music, and dance. Learn to play the island's traditional instruments, try your hand at crafting local artwork, or join a dance class to move to the beat of Bonairean rhythms.

Celebrate diversity and unity in Bonaire's multicultural society, where indigenous, African, European, and Caribbean influences blend harmoniously. Whether you're exploring historical sites, enjoying local cuisine, participating in festivals, or learning traditional crafts, cultural experiences in Bonaire promise to enrich your journey and leave you with lasting memories.

Immerse yourself in the essence of Bonaire's culture, where every encounter is an opportunity to connect with its people, traditions, and way of life. Embrace the warmth of Bonairean hospitality, celebrate its cultural diversity, and discover the island's soul through its vibrant cultural experiences.

Local Festivals and Events in Bonaire

Immerse yourself in the vibrant culture of Bonaire by exploring its local festivals and events. Throughout the year, the island comes alive with celebrations that showcase its rich heritage, traditions, and community spirit. Let's take a look at some of the most notable events:

1. Carnival:
Bonaire's Carnival, typically held in February or March, is a lively extravaganza of music, dance, and colorful parades. Join locals and visitors alike in experiencing vibrant costumes, rhythmic music from local bands, and the energetic Tumba dance competitions. It's a must-attend event for those seeking an authentic taste of Bonairean culture.

2. Simadan:
Celebrated in April, Simadan is Bonaire's harvest festival, highlighting the island's agricultural roots. Experience traditional folk music, lively dance performances, and

participate in activities like the Kant'i Hubentut (youth song and dance competition). It's a wonderful opportunity to learn about Bonaire's farming traditions and sample local dishes made from freshly harvested produce.

3. Dia di Rincon:
Dia di Rincon, held annually on April 30th, is a cherished cultural event that celebrates the history and traditions of Rincon, Bonaire's oldest village. Join in the festivities featuring traditional music, dance performances, local crafts, and delicious food. The event offers a glimpse into the island's rural life and strong sense of community.

4. Bonaire International Sailing Regatta:
Sailing enthusiasts shouldn't miss the Bonaire International Sailing Regatta, typically held in October. This event attracts sailors from around the world to compete in various races amidst Bonaire's stunning turquoise waters. Spectators can enjoy the competitive spirit, as well as shoreside festivities including live music, food stalls, and cultural performances.

5. Dive Festival:
For underwater enthusiasts, the Bonaire Dive Festival in June is a highlight. This event celebrates Bonaire's reputation as a top diving destination with guided dives, underwater photography workshops, conservation activities, and marine life presentations. It's an ideal

opportunity to explore the island's pristine reefs and participate in efforts to preserve its marine ecosystem.

Attending local festivals and events not only offers memorable experiences but also provides deeper insights into Bonaire's culture and traditions. For more information on event dates and activities, visit Bonaire Event Calendar.
(www. infobonaire.com/bonaire-event-calendar)
Plan your visit around these festivities to fully immerse yourself in the island's vibrant spirit. Embrace the opportunity to interact with locals, savor traditional cuisine, and create lasting memories during your Bonaire adventure.

Museums and Historical Sites

In Bonaire, museums and historical sites offer glimpses into the island's rich past and culture. One notable site is the Bonaire Museum of Natural History, located in the capital city of Kralendijk. Here, you can explore exhibits showcasing the island's unique geology, flora, and fauna. It's a great place to learn about the diverse ecosystems that make Bonaire so special.

For those interested in the island's maritime history, the Bonaire Maritime Museum is a must-visit. Housed in an old plantation house, this museum tells the story of Bonaire's relationship with the sea, from its fishing traditions to its role in the salt industry. You can see artifacts, models of old ships, and learn about the local sailors who braved the Caribbean waters.

If you're keen to explore Bonaire's colonial past, visit the Mangazina di Rei. Located in Rincon, Bonaire's oldest town, this historical site was once a storehouse for goods shipped from the Netherlands. Today, it's a museum where you can discover more about the island's early settlers, their struggles, and their cultural contributions.

For a deeper dive into Bonaire's slave history, head to the Cadushy Distillery and Museum. While primarily known for its distillery, where you can taste locally made rum, the museum also sheds light on Bonaire's history of slavery and the resilience of the African-Bonairean community.

Each of these sites offers a unique perspective on Bonaire's past and present. Whether you're interested in natural history, maritime adventures, colonial heritage, or cultural insights, exploring these museums and historical sites will enrich your understanding of this beautiful island. They are not only educational but also provide a deeper connection to Bonaire's rich cultural tapestry.

Art Galleries and Local Crafts

In Bonaire, art galleries and local crafts showcase the island's creativity and cultural expressions. Visiting these places gives you a glimpse into the vibrant artistic community here.

One of the must-visit spots is Kas di Arte, located in Kralendijk. This gallery features works by local artists, including paintings, sculptures, and crafts that reflect Bonairean life and landscapes. It's a great place to appreciate the island's artistic talent and perhaps even purchase a unique piece as a souvenir.

For those interested in local crafts, Mangazina di Artesania Boneriano in Rincon is a treasure trove. Here, artisans showcase traditional crafts such as handmade pottery, woven baskets, and intricately crafted jewelry. You can watch them work and learn about the techniques passed down through generations.

Another notable gallery is the Cinnamon Art Gallery, also in Kralendijk. This gallery exhibits contemporary artworks by both local and international artists. It's a space where modern art meets the Caribbean vibe, offering a diverse range of paintings, sculptures, and mixed-media creations.

If you're exploring the southern part of the island, don't miss the Terra Art Projects in Belnem. This gallery focuses on environmental and social themes through art, often featuring exhibitions that raise awareness about sustainability and conservation efforts in Bonaire.

Visiting these art galleries and local craft shops not only supports the local economy but also allows you to connect with Bonaire's artistic soul. Whether you're an art enthusiast or simply curious about the island's cultural heritage, these places offer a delightful and enriching experience.

CHAPTER 8.

DINING AND NIGHTLIFE

Bonaire's dining and nightlife scene offers a delightful fusion of flavors and experiences that cater to every palate and preference. From charming seaside eateries to lively bars and restaurants, the island beckons visitors to indulge in its culinary delights and vibrant nocturnal offerings.

In Bonaire, dining is not just a meal; it's an experience. Imagine dining al fresco with the gentle sea breeze as your companion, savoring freshly caught seafood prepared with local spices and herbs that tantalize your taste buds. Many restaurants pride themselves on using fresh, locally sourced ingredients, ensuring that each dish reflects the island's bountiful natural resources and rich culinary heritage.

Whether you're craving Caribbean cuisine, international flavors, or a taste of fusion dishes, Bonaire's restaurants deliver with creativity and flair. From casual beachfront cafes to upscale dining establishments, there's something to suit every occasion and budget.

As the sun sets, Bonaire's nightlife comes alive with a diverse array of options. You can start your evening with sunset cocktails at a beach bar, where the view is as refreshing as the drinks. Live music fills the air at many venues, offering a laid-back atmosphere where you can unwind and mingle with locals and fellow travelers alike.

For those seeking a livelier scene, Bonaire offers several bars and clubs where you can dance the night away to Caribbean beats, reggae rhythms, or contemporary tunes spun by local DJs. Whether you prefer a cozy lounge setting or a bustling dance floor under the stars, the island's nightlife promises unforgettable moments and vibrant energy.

Beyond the dining and nightlife establishments, Bonaire also hosts special events throughout the year that showcase its culinary prowess and festive spirit. Food festivals, wine tastings, and cultural celebrations often feature prominently on the island's calendar, providing opportunities to delve deeper into Bonaire's gastronomic and social scene.

In this chapter, we'll explore the best dining spots, hidden gems, nightlife hotspots, and cultural events that make Bonaire a paradise for food enthusiasts and night owls alike. Get ready to embark on a flavorful journey and discover the vibrant nightlife that awaits you on this enchanting Caribbean island.

Top Restaurants

When it comes to dining on Bonaire, you're in for a treat with a variety of restaurants offering delicious meals in stunning settings. One standout is It Rains Fishes. Located right on the waterfront in Kralendijk, this restaurant not only boasts fresh seafood but also mesmerizing views of the Caribbean Sea. I remember enjoying a delightful evening there, starting with a sunset cocktail on their terrace while watching boats bobbing gently in the harbor. The menu featured local fish dishes prepared with a creative twist, accompanied by sides bursting with Caribbean flavors.

Another gem is At Sea Restaurant, tucked away in a charming garden setting just outside of town. Getting there was easy; a short drive from Kralendijk led me to this oasis of culinary delights. The ambiance was relaxed yet elegant, perfect for a romantic dinner or a gathering with friends. The menu highlighted a fusion of Caribbean and international cuisines, and I savored every bite of their seafood platter, which included freshly caught lobster and shrimp.

For a more casual vibe, Bobbejan's BBQ is a must-visit. Located at No. 2 Kaya Albert Engelhardt, Kralendijk, this open-air eatery specializes in grilled meats and local favorites. I loved the laid-back atmosphere, where diners can sink their toes into the sand while enjoying a hearty barbecue meal. It's a great spot to mingle with locals and other travelers, sharing stories over plates of tender ribs and savory sides.

Each restaurant offers a unique dining experience, from breathtaking views to flavors that celebrate Bonaire's culinary diversity. Whether you're a food enthusiast or simply looking to unwind with good food and company, Bonaire's top restaurants promise an unforgettable dining experience that captures the essence of island life.

Local Cuisine and Must-Try Dishes

Local cuisine often reflects the cultural richness and traditions of a region. Here are five dishes from around the world that are worth trying:

1. Kibbeling (Netherlands): Kibbeling is a Dutch street food made of bite-sized pieces of battered and fried fish, typically served with a side of garlic sauce. My first taste of kibbeling at a local market in Amsterdam was a delightful surprise - crispy and savory, perfect for a quick bite while exploring the city.

2. Poutine (Canada): Originating from Quebec, poutine consists of French fries topped with cheese curds and smothered in gravy. Trying poutine for the first time in Montreal was a comforting experience - the combination

of crispy fries, melty cheese, and savory gravy was truly satisfying.

3. Paella (Spain): Paella is a Spanish rice dish cooked with saffron, seafood, chicken, and vegetables. Enjoying paella in Valencia was a feast for the senses - the vibrant colors and aromatic saffron infused every bite with a rich, flavorful taste of Spain.

4. Sushi (Japan): Sushi is a Japanese dish of vinegared rice combined with seafood, vegetables, and sometimes tropical fruits. My first sushi experience in Tokyo was unforgettable - the freshness of the fish, the delicate balance of flavors, and the artistry in presentation made it a culinary journey.

5. Tacos al Pastor (Mexico): Tacos al Pastor are a popular Mexican street food made with marinated pork cooked on a vertical spit, served on corn tortillas with pineapple, onions, cilantro, and salsa. Trying tacos al Pastor in Mexico City was a sensory delight - the juicy, flavorful pork combined with the sweetness of pineapple created a delicious explosion of taste.

Health Tips for Allergies and Restrictions:
- If you have seafood allergies, be cautious with dishes like paella or sushi that contain seafood. Always ask about ingredients.

- For gluten sensitivity, watch out for soy sauce in sushi and other dishes. Look for gluten-free options or substitutes.
- If you're lactose intolerant, be aware of cheese and dairy-based sauces like those in poutine. Ask for dairy-free alternatives.
- Vegetarians and vegans can enjoy sushi with vegetable fillings or tacos al Pastor with grilled vegetables instead of meat.

Exploring local cuisine allows you to immerse yourself in the culture and flavors of a place. Remember to savor each dish and appreciate the unique culinary traditions that each region has to offer.

Bars and Nightlife Spots

Karel's Beach Bar is located right by the sea, offering a relaxed atmosphere with stunning sunset views. It's a favorite among locals and tourists alike for its laid-back ambiance and delicious cocktails. Sip on your drink while feeling the gentle sea breeze—a perfect way to end the day.

Little Havana brings a taste of Cuban flair with lively music and Cuban-inspired cocktails. This vibrant bar is ideal for dancing to salsa music or enjoying the upbeat atmosphere with friends.

City Café Bonaire, located in Kralendijk, offers a cozy spot with a diverse menu of drinks, including local beers and specialty cocktails. Its outdoor terrace is great for people-watching while enjoying a refreshing beverage.

Boudoir Bonaire provides a sophisticated evening with craft cocktails and an elegant setting. It's perfect for a special night out or a romantic date in a chic lounge atmosphere.

Liquor Store Bonaire offers a unique concept where you can purchase your favorite bottle of liquor and enjoy it onsite with friends. It's a relaxed setting with a wide selection of drinks and a laid-back atmosphere.

When exploring Bonaire's nightlife, remember to pace yourself and drink responsibly. Each bar and nightlife spot has its own charm and vibe, so feel free to explore different places to find your favorite hangout. Whether you prefer dancing to live music or savoring cocktails by the ocean, Bonaire offers something for everyone to enjoy after dark.

Food Markets and Street Food

Food markets and street food are vibrant parts of Bonaire's culinary scene, offering a variety of local flavors and fresh produce. Here's a look at what you can expect:

1. Krioyo Market: Located in Kralendijk, Krioyo Market is a bustling hub where locals and tourists alike gather to shop for fresh fruits, vegetables, and local delicacies. You can find everything from ripe mangoes and papayas to freshly caught fish and spices that add a kick to your dishes.

2. Rincon Market: In the heart of Rincon, Bonaire's oldest town, this market is a cultural experience in itself. Open on Saturdays, it offers a glimpse into traditional island life. You can sample homemade snacks like pastechis (savory pastries filled with cheese or meat) and karko (conch) soup.

3. Food Trucks and Stands: Throughout the island, especially near popular beaches and tourist spots, you'll find colorful food trucks and stands offering local street food. Try dishes like kabritu stoba (goat stew), fresh ceviche made from locally caught fish, or crispy keshi yena (stuffed cheese) prepared with a variety of fillings.

4. Local Snacks: Don't miss out on trying pan bati, a traditional cornmeal pancake served with a variety of

toppings such as cheese, ham, or even peanut butter. It's a favorite snack among locals and visitors alike.

Exploring food markets and trying street food in Bonaire is not just about eating—it's about immersing yourself in the island's culture and flavors. You'll find friendly vendors eager to share their favorite dishes and culinary traditions. Just remember to bring cash, as many of these markets and food stalls may not accept credit cards. Enjoy sampling the diverse tastes of Bonaire while soaking in the island's laid-back atmosphere!

CHAPTER 9.

SHOPPING

Welcome to the vibrant world of shopping in Bonaire! Whether you're looking for unique souvenirs, local handicrafts, or everyday essentials, the island offers a variety of shopping experiences to suit every taste and budget.

Bonaire's shopping scene is as diverse as its culture and landscapes. From quaint boutiques and art galleries to bustling markets and modern shopping centers, you'll find a treasure trove of goods waiting to be discovered.

Local artisans showcase their talents through handmade jewelry, pottery, and artwork inspired by the island's natural beauty. Dive shops offer top-notch gear for underwater adventures, while specialty stores stock everything from Caribbean spices to locally produced honey and hot sauces.

Shopping in Bonaire isn't just about acquiring goods—it's a chance to connect with the island's rich heritage and support local businesses. Whether you're browsing through the colorful stalls of a street market or exploring air-conditioned malls, each shopping excursion promises a new discovery and a glimpse into the island's unique charm.

So, start grabbing your shopping list and get ready to explore Bonaire's markets, boutiques, and more. Whether you're seeking a memorable souvenir or simply indulging in some retail therapy, Bonaire invites you to shop to your heart's content and take a piece of its magic home with you.

Best Shopping Areas

When it comes to shopping in Bonaire, you'll find a range of vibrant areas offering unique experiences and diverse products.

Kralendijk is the capital city and a bustling hub for shopping. Along the waterfront promenade, you'll discover a mix of local boutiques, souvenir shops, and jewelry stores. Here, you can find everything from handmade crafts to stylish clothing and accessories.

Kaya Grandi is another charming street in Kralendijk known for its vibrant atmosphere and diverse shops. Wander along Kaya Grandi to explore art galleries showcasing local talent, quaint cafes offering Caribbean treats, and stores selling island-inspired gifts.

Rincon, Bonaire's oldest village, offers a more traditional shopping experience. Visit the local market to sample fresh produce, handmade goods, and local snacks. You'll also find small shops selling handicrafts, artwork, and souvenirs that highlight Bonairean culture.

Plaza Beach Resort Bonaire, located near the southern tip of the island, features a shopping area with boutique stores. Here, you can browse for unique clothing, beachwear, and accessories, perfect for enjoying the island's sunny climate.

For luxury shopping, head to the Harbour Village Marina area. This upscale spot features boutique shops offering designer clothing, fine jewelry, and high-end home decor items. Enjoy strolling around the marina while admiring yachts and soaking in the scenic views.

Throughout Bonaire, various craft markets offer opportunities to support local artisans. These markets are ideal for picking up authentic souvenirs such as pottery, woven goods, and artwork that reflect the island's culture and traditions.

Exploring these shopping areas allows you to experience the vibrant local culture of Bonaire while finding unique treasures to take home as mementos of your visit.

Souvenirs to Buy

1. Local Artwork: Look for paintings, sculptures, and handmade crafts created by local artists. These pieces often reflect the vibrant colors and natural beauty of Bonaire.

2. Sea Salt: Bonaire is renowned for its high-quality sea salt harvested from salt pans. You can find packaged sea salt in various flavors, perfect for seasoning dishes or as a unique gift.

3. Delft Blue Pottery: Inspired by Dutch colonial heritage, Delft Blue pottery is a popular souvenir. It often features intricate blue designs on white ceramic, reflecting both European and Caribbean influences.

4. Bonairean Rum: Explore local distilleries and bring back a bottle of Bonairean rum. Whether dark or spiced, Bonairean rum makes for a flavorful souvenir or a delightful gift for friends.

5. Cactus Liqueur: Made from locally grown cactus fruit, this liqueur offers a taste of Bonaire's unique flora. Its sweet and tangy flavor profile makes it a memorable souvenir to savor.

6. Bonairean Hot Sauces: Spicy food enthusiasts will appreciate Bonaire's hot sauces, crafted from local chili

peppers. These sauces range from mildly spicy to intensely hot, offering a taste of Caribbean heat.

7. Jewelry: Look for jewelry pieces crafted from Bonaire's distinctive black coral, often shaped into earrings, necklaces, and bracelets. These pieces showcase the island's marine beauty.

8. Seashell and Coral Crafts: Handmade items such as wind chimes, picture frames, and ornaments crafted from seashells and coral make for charming souvenirs that capture Bonaire's coastal charm.

9. T-shirts and Clothing: Take home a Bonaire-themed T-shirt or casual wear featuring island motifs and vibrant colors. These items are practical and serve as wearable mementos of your trip.

10. Caribbean Spices: Bring home a taste of Bonaire with Caribbean spice blends, such as jerk seasoning or curry mixes. These spices add an authentic Caribbean flavor to your culinary creations.

Shopping for souvenirs in Bonaire not only allows you to bring home a piece of the island's culture but also supports local artisans and businesses. Whether you're seeking artwork, local delicacies, or unique handicrafts, you're sure to find the perfect souvenir to commemorate your time in Bonaire.

Local Markets

Local markets in Bonaire offer a vibrant and authentic shopping experience where you can explore local flavors and crafts. Here's what you can expect:

1. Kralendijk's Floating Market: This market, located along the waterfront in Kralendijk, is famous for its fresh produce and seafood brought in by Venezuelan vendors on boats. It's a lively scene where you can find tropical fruits, vegetables, and sometimes handmade crafts.

2. Rincon Art Market: Held in the historic village of Rincon, this market showcases local artwork, handicrafts, and traditional Bonairean souvenirs. You'll find paintings, sculptures, pottery, and jewelry crafted by local artists, offering a glimpse into the island's cultural heritage.

3. Cultural Market in Wilhelmina Park: Located in Kralendijk's Wilhelmina Park, this market features stalls selling handmade goods, clothing, accessories, and local snacks. It's a great place to pick up gifts or indulge in some local treats while enjoying views of the Caribbean Sea.

4. Terramar Museum Craft Market: Adjacent to the Terramar Museum in Kralendijk, this market offers a selection of local crafts, including woven baskets,

woodcarvings, and seashell ornaments. It's an ideal spot to support local artisans and discover unique souvenirs.

5. Renowned Supermarkets: While not traditional markets, supermarkets like Van den Tweel and Cultimara in Kralendijk offer a variety of locally produced goods alongside international products. You can find everything from fresh fruits and vegetables to Bonairean hot sauces and spices.

Visiting these markets not only allows you to shop for authentic Bonairean products but also gives you a chance to interact with locals and immerse yourself in the island's vibrant culture. Whether you're looking for fresh ingredients, handmade crafts, or unique souvenirs, Bonaire's local markets provide a delightful shopping experience that enhances your stay on the island.

CHAPTER 10.

Day Trips and Excursions

One of the most exciting aspects of visiting Bonaire is the variety of day trips and excursions available to explore. Whether you're drawn to the allure of nearby islands, the thrill of boat tours, the excitement of adventure tours, or the richness of cultural excursions, there's something for every traveler. In this chapter, I'll take you through some of the best experiences you can have beyond the main island, providing insider tips to make the most of your time. These adventures promise to add a whole new dimension to your Bonaire trip, creating memories that will last a lifetime. Let's dive into the diverse activities that await you just beyond the shores of Bonaire.

Exploring Nearby Islands

Nearby islands to Bonaire offer unique experiences that add to the charm of a Caribbean getaway. Exploring these islands provides a chance to see diverse landscapes, enjoy different activities, and immerse yourself in various cultures.

First, there's Curaçao, just a short flight away from Bonaire. Curaçao is known for its vibrant capital, Willemstad, with its colorful Dutch colonial architecture and floating Queen Emma Bridge. The island is a haven for divers and snorkelers, with its clear waters and abundant marine life. Visiting Curaçao, make sure to explore the Hato Caves and relax on the stunning beaches like Kenepa Beach.

Another nearby island is Aruba, which is about a 40-minute flight from Bonaire. Aruba is famous for its white sandy beaches, such as Eagle Beach and Palm Beach, where you can enjoy water sports or simply relax under the sun. The island also offers exciting activities like visiting the Arikok National Park, exploring the Casibari Rock Formations, or trying your luck at one of the many casinos.

Klein Curaçao is a small, uninhabited island southeast of Curaçao. It's perfect for a day trip from Curaçao. Known for its stunning beaches and crystal-clear waters, it's a great spot for snorkeling, diving, or just relaxing. The island is also home to a historic lighthouse and shipwrecks, adding a bit of adventure to your visit.

Another interesting destination is Isla Margarita, located off the coast of Venezuela. This island is a bit further, but it's known for its beautiful beaches and vibrant nightlife. Playa El Agua and Playa Parguito are popular beaches where you can enjoy water activities or relax by the shore. The island also has shopping areas and cultural sites, such as the Castillo de San Carlos de Borromeo.

There's Los Roques, an archipelago of Venezuela. It's a paradise for nature lovers and water sports enthusiasts. With its pristine beaches, clear waters, and abundant marine life, Los Roques offers excellent opportunities for fishing, diving, and snorkeling. The main island, Gran Roque, has charming inns and restaurants where you can enjoy local seafood dishes.

Visiting these nearby islands from Bonaire is easy and rewarding. Each island offers its unique charm and a variety of activities, making them perfect for day trips or longer stays. By exploring these destinations, you can enrich your Caribbean experience and create unforgettable memories.

Boat Tours

Boat tours in Bonaire are a fantastic way to explore the island's stunning coastline, crystal-clear waters, and vibrant marine life. Whether you're looking for adventure or a relaxing day on the water, there are various options to suit your preferences.

One popular boat tour is a snorkeling trip to Klein Bonaire. This uninhabited island just off the coast of Bonaire is surrounded by pristine coral reefs teeming with colorful fish. The journey to Klein Bonaire is a treat in itself, with stunning views of the coastline and the opportunity to spot dolphins playing in the waves. Once you arrive, you'll be greeted by pristine beaches and crystal-clear waters teeming with marine life. Snorkeling here is an unforgettable experience, with vibrant coral reefs and a diverse array of fish just below the surface. Most tours depart from Kralendijk, the main town on Bonaire, and include all the necessary snorkeling gear.

For a more luxurious experience, consider a sunset sailing tour. These tours typically involve cruising along the coast of Bonaire as the sun sets over the Caribbean Sea. Many sunset tours include drinks and snacks, making it a perfect way to unwind and enjoy the stunning views. The warm breeze, the sound of the waves, and the vibrant colors of the sunset create a magical atmosphere.

If you're interested in marine life, a glass-bottom boat tour is an excellent choice. These tours allow you to see the underwater world without getting wet. The boats have large glass panels in the bottom, offering clear views of the coral reefs and marine creatures below. It's a great option for families with children or anyone who prefers to stay dry while exploring the underwater beauty of Bonaire.

Fishing enthusiasts can opt for a fishing charter. Bonaire's waters are rich with fish, and a fishing tour can be a thrilling experience. Whether you're an experienced angler or a beginner, the local guides will provide you with the necessary equipment and tips. You can try your hand at catching various species, and some tours even offer the option to cook and enjoy your catch on board.

For those who want a more personalized experience, private boat charters are available. Renting a private boat allows you to customize your itinerary, choose your destinations, and enjoy a more intimate setting. Whether you want to explore secluded beaches, snorkel at your own pace, or simply relax on the water, a private charter can cater to your specific desires.

When choosing a boat tour, it's essential to consider a few tips. First, book your tour in advance, especially during peak tourist seasons, to ensure availability. Second, don't forget to bring essentials such as sunscreen, a hat, sunglasses, and a reusable water bottle. Lastly, if you're prone to seasickness, consider taking medication before the trip to ensure a more comfortable experience.

Boat tours in Bonaire offer a unique and memorable way to experience the island's natural beauty. Whether you're snorkeling, sailing at sunset, observing marine life through a glass-bottom boat, fishing, or enjoying a private charter, there's something for everyone. These tours provide an opportunity to see Bonaire from a different perspective and create lasting memories of your visit to this Caribbean paradise.

Adventure Tours

Adventure tours in Bonaire offer an exciting way to explore the island's diverse landscapes and vibrant culture. Whether you're an adrenaline junkie or simply looking for a unique way to experience the island, there's something for everyone.

One of the most popular adventure tours is a guided ATV (All-Terrain Vehicle) tour. These tours take you off the beaten path to explore Bonaire's rugged terrain. You'll drive through rocky trails, past cacti and unique geological formations, and reach stunning viewpoints where you can see the island's coastline from a new perspective. The tours usually start in Kralendijk, and the guides provide all the necessary safety gear and instructions. It's a thrilling way to see parts of Bonaire that are otherwise inaccessible.

For those who enjoy being on the water, a kayaking tour in Bonaire's mangroves is a must. The mangrove forests are a crucial part of the island's ecosystem, and kayaking through these serene waters allows you to get up close to the flora and fauna. You might spot birds, fish, and other wildlife as you paddle through the calm channels. The tours are generally easy and suitable for all levels of kayakers. They often begin at Lac Bay, where guides will provide kayaks and safety equipment.

Caving tours offer another exciting adventure. Bonaire is home to several limestone caves, some of which are open for guided tours. Inside the caves, you'll see impressive stalactites and stalagmites, as well as ancient rock formations. Some tours even include the chance to swim in underground pools. The guides provide helmets and flashlights, ensuring a safe and enjoyable experience. These tours usually require a bit of physical activity, such as climbing and crawling, but the breathtaking sights inside the caves make it all worthwhile.

If you prefer to stay above ground but still want an adventure, consider a mountain biking tour. Bonaire has a network of trails suitable for different skill levels, from easy rides along the coast to challenging routes through the hills. A guided tour will take you to the best spots, whether it's a scenic ride along the beach or a more intense trek through the island's interior. Bikes and helmets are provided, and the guides will ensure you have a fun and safe experience.

For those who love the ocean, a windsurfing or kitesurfing lesson is a fantastic way to experience Bonaire's famous winds and waves. Lac Bay is the go-to spot for these activities, with its shallow waters and steady winds providing ideal conditions. Local schools offer lessons for beginners and advanced surfers alike. The instructors are experienced and patient, ensuring you get the hang of it quickly. Windsurfing and kitesurfing are exhilarating ways to enjoy the beautiful waters of Bonaire while getting a great workout.

When planning an adventure tour, it's important to book in advance, especially during the high season. Wear comfortable clothing and shoes suitable for the activity, and don't forget to bring sunscreen, a hat, and plenty of water. Most importantly, be ready to have an amazing time exploring Bonaire's natural beauty and getting your adrenaline pumping.

Adventure tours in Bonaire provide a thrilling way to discover the island's diverse landscapes. Whether you're driving an ATV through rugged terrain, kayaking through mangroves, exploring caves, mountain biking, or windsurfing, there's no shortage of exciting activities to choose from. These tours offer unique experiences and create unforgettable memories of your time on this beautiful Caribbean island.

Itineraries

Explore Bonaire with these carefully curated itineraries. Whether you have a few days or two weeks, this section will help you make the most of your stay, from stunning beaches and world-class diving to vibrant culture and thrilling outdoor activities.

1-3 Days: A Quick Escape

Day 1: Arrival

Morning: Arrive at Flamingo International Airport, greeted by warm breezes and clear skies. Check into your cozy hotel in Kralendijk, the lively capital.

Afternoon: Stroll along Kralendijk's waterfront, where colorful buildings line the streets. Stop at local cafes to try island specialties like fish stew or a refreshing fruit smoothie.

Evening: Watch the sun dip into the Caribbean Sea as you dine at a seaside restaurant, enjoying fresh seafood and the gentle lapping of waves.

Day 2: Snorkeling and Cultural Exploration
Morning: Take a short boat ride to Klein Bonaire for snorkeling. Glide through turquoise waters, marveling at

coral reefs teeming with colorful fish and maybe even spot a sea turtle.

Afternoon: Visit the Bonaire Museum to learn about the island's history, from its early settlers to the days of salt mining. Explore exhibits showcasing local crafts and artifacts.
Evening: Attend a local event to experience Bonaire's culture firsthand, with music, dance, and delicious local snacks.

Day 3: Outdoor Adventures and Departure

Morning: Explore Washington Slagbaai National Park's trails. Hike through desert landscapes dotted with cacti, enjoying views of rugged coastlines and secluded beaches.

Afternoon: Relax on a quiet beach or explore Kralendijk's shops for souvenirs. Take in the last views of Bonaire's natural beauty before heading home.

Departure: Depart with memories of Bonaire's warm hospitality and natural wonders, already planning your return to this laid-back island paradise.

4-7 Days: Deep Dive into Bonaire's Wonders

Day 4-5: Water Adventures and Relaxation

Morning: Start each day with snorkeling at different spots like Salt Pier or Andrea I and II wrecks. Discover underwater worlds alive with colorful fish and intricate coral formations.

Afternoon: Afternoons are for sunbathing on Sorobon Beach or exploring local markets for handmade crafts and tasty treats like pastechi (local pastries).

Evening: Enjoy dinner at a beachside restaurant, savoring grilled fish or a hearty local stew.

Day 6: Windsurfing and Kitesurfing

Morning: Head to Sorobon Beach for windsurfing or kitesurfing lessons. Feel the thrill of gliding across shallow waters, guided by warm trade winds.

Afternoon: Visit Gotomeer to see pink flamingos wading in the shallows, a serene reminder of Bonaire's natural beauty and conservation efforts.

Evening: Watch the sunset from a boat cruise, enjoying the peaceful colors reflecting on the water.

Day 7: Nature and Farewell

Morning: Trek through Washington Slagbaai National Park, climbing Mount Brandaris for panoramic views of the island and its surrounding seas.

Afternoon: Explore Rincon, Bonaire's oldest town. Wander its narrow streets, stopping at local galleries and cafes to immerse yourself in island life.
Departure: Leave Bonaire with a heart full of memories, knowing you've experienced the best of this Caribbean gem.

8-14 Days: Immersive Exploration and Relaxation

Day 8-10: Cultural and Historical Highlights

Morning: Dive deeper into Bonaire's history with visits to landmarks like Cadushy Distillery and the Slavery Museum in Rincon.

Afternoon: Relax on secluded beaches like Bachelor's Beach or explore the island's diverse ecosystems on guided nature tours.

Evening: Sample local cuisine at traditional eateries, with flavors blending Dutch and Caribbean influences.
Day 11-12: Extended Diving and Snorkeling

Morning: Spend mornings diving into Bonaire's famed dive sites, from the "1000 Steps" to the wreck dives off Klein Bonaire. Encounter diverse marine life in clear Caribbean waters.

Afternoon: Participate in eco-tours focused on marine conservation or simply relax with beachfront yoga sessions.

Evening: Attend local festivals or music performances, celebrating Bonaire's culture and community.

Day 13-14: Relaxation and Reflection

Morning: Mornings begin with paddleboarding or hiking along coastal trails. Take in the sights and sounds of Bonaire's natural landscapes.

Afternoon: Indulge in spa treatments or local art workshops, gaining insights into Bonaire's creative spirit.

Evening: Enjoy a farewell dinner under the stars, reflecting on your time in Bonaire and dreaming of future adventures.

CHAPTER 10.

PRACTICAL INFORMATION AND RESOURCES

When planning a trip to Bonaire, having practical information at your fingertips is essential for a smooth and enjoyable experience. This chapter is dedicated to providing you with all the necessary details you need to know before and during your stay on the island. From travel tips to local customs, health precautions, and safety advice, understanding the practical aspects of your journey will help ensure that your time in Bonaire is as stress-free as possible.

First, let's talk about travel essentials. It's important to be aware of the entry requirements for Bonaire, including necessary travel documents and visas. Knowing what to pack is also crucial, especially given the island's warm, tropical climate. Lightweight, breathable clothing is recommended, along with sun protection like hats, sunglasses, and sunscreen.

Once you arrive on the island, you'll need to know how to get around. Information on transportation options, including car rentals, taxis, and public transportation, can help you navigate Bonaire efficiently. Understanding local driving laws and regulations, as well as having a reliable map or GPS system, will make exploring the island much easier.

Accommodation is another key aspect of your trip. Whether you're staying in a hotel, guesthouse, or vacation rental, it's useful to know the amenities and services available, as well as tips for making your stay comfortable. Additionally, familiarizing yourself with the local currency, banking services, and the availability of ATMs will help you manage your finances while on the island.

Health and safety are paramount when traveling. Knowing where to find medical facilities and pharmacies, as well as understanding local health regulations and vaccinations, can provide peace of mind. Safety tips, including how to stay secure while exploring the island and what to do in case of emergencies, are also crucial for a worry-free trip.

Understanding local customs and etiquette can enhance your experience and help you connect more deeply with Bonairean culture. Learning a few basic phrases in Papiamento, the local language, can go a long way in showing respect and building rapport with residents. Being aware of cultural norms, such as appropriate dress codes and social behaviors, will also help you blend in more seamlessly.

It's helpful to know about communication options while in Bonaire. Information on mobile phone usage, internet availability, and where to find Wi-Fi hotspots can keep you connected with family and friends back home. Additionally, knowing the locations of tourist information centers can provide you with resources and assistance during your stay.

Being well-prepared with practical information can significantly enhance your visit to Bonaire. By understanding travel essentials, transportation options, accommodation details, health and safety tips, local customs, and communication options, you'll be equipped to make the most of your time on this beautiful island. This chapter aims to provide you with all the necessary knowledge to ensure a smooth, enjoyable, and memorable trip to Bonaire.

Currency and Banks

Understanding currency matters in Bonaire is essential for a smooth and hassle-free trip. In Bonaire, the official currency is the US Dollar (USD), which makes it convenient for travelers from the United States.

When you arrive on the island, you'll find that most businesses, including hotels, restaurants, and shops, accept major credit and debit cards. However, it's always a good idea to carry some cash for smaller establishments or activities where cards might not be accepted. ATMs are widely available in the main towns and at the airport, allowing you to withdraw cash as needed. Most ATMs accept international cards, but it's wise to inform your bank of your travel plans to avoid any issues.

Exchanging currency is straightforward since the US Dollar is the standard. If you need to exchange other currencies, it's best to do so at major banks or at the airport upon arrival. Banks typically offer better exchange rates than hotels or currency exchange kiosks. The main banks in Bonaire are MCB Bonaire, RBC Royal Bank, and Girobank. These banks provide various services, including currency exchange, ATM access, and assistance with financial matters. Their branches are usually open from Monday to Friday, with some banks also open on Saturday mornings.

Using credit and debit cards is generally safe in Bonaire, but it's always good practice to check with your bank regarding foreign transaction fees. Some cards offer travel benefits, such as no foreign transaction fees, which can save you money. It's also advisable to carry multiple forms of payment in case one method isn't accepted.

For those planning to stay in Bonaire for an extended period or conducting business, opening a local bank account might be beneficial. The process usually requires identification, proof of address, and an initial deposit. It's best to visit the bank in person to understand the specific requirements and options available.

When shopping or dining, it's customary to tip around 10-15% for good service. Some restaurants may include a service charge, so check your bill to see if a tip is already included. For smaller purchases, such as snacks or souvenirs, having smaller denominations of cash can be handy.

Managing your finances in Bonaire is relatively easy thanks to the use of the US Dollar, the availability of ATMs, and the widespread acceptance of credit and debit cards. By carrying a mix of payment methods and understanding local banking options, you'll be well-prepared to handle your expenses and enjoy your time on the island without any financial worries.

Language and Communication

When visiting Bonaire, understanding the language and communication aspects can enhance your travel experience. The official languages of Bonaire are Dutch and Papiamentu, but English and Spanish are also widely spoken. This multilingual environment makes it easier for visitors to communicate with locals.

Papiamentu is a Creole language that blends elements of Spanish, Portuguese, Dutch, African languages, and Arawakan. It is commonly used in everyday conversations and has a warm, rhythmic sound. Learning a few basic phrases in Papiamentu, such as "Bon dia" (Good morning), "Bon tardi" (Good afternoon), and "Danki" (Thank you), can be a delightful way to connect with locals and show appreciation for their culture.

English is spoken by nearly everyone in Bonaire, especially in tourist areas, hotels, restaurants, and shops. This makes it easy for English-speaking visitors to ask for directions, order food, and interact with service staff. Many signs, menus, and informational materials are also available in English, ensuring clear communication.

Spanish is also widely spoken, given the island's proximity to Spanish-speaking countries. If you speak Spanish, you'll find it easy to communicate with many locals who are bilingual. This can be especially helpful in areas less frequented by tourists.

Mobile phone coverage in Bonaire is reliable, and most international cell phone carriers offer roaming services. However, to avoid high roaming charges, consider purchasing a local SIM card upon arrival. Local providers like Digicel and TELBO offer prepaid plans with data, which can be useful for navigation, staying connected, and accessing information.

Internet access is widely available, with most hotels, restaurants, and cafes offering free Wi-Fi. This makes it easy to stay in touch with friends and family, share your travel experiences on social media, and look up information about attractions and activities.

For more formal communication, such as making reservations or seeking assistance from authorities, knowing a bit of Dutch can be beneficial, but it is not essential. English is typically sufficient for most needs.

If you need help or information, don't hesitate to ask locals. People in Bonaire are generally friendly and willing to assist visitors. Whether you're asking for directions, recommendations, or simply engaging in a friendly chat, you'll find that communication is straightforward and welcoming.

Language and communication in Bonaire are easy to navigate, thanks to the widespread use of English and the friendly, multilingual population. By learning a few phrases in Papiamentu and taking advantage of modern communication tools, you'll be well-equipped to enjoy your stay and connect with the local culture.

Emergency Contacts

When traveling to Bonaire, it's important to know the emergency contacts and how to reach help quickly if needed. Here's a guide to the essential emergency contacts you should have on hand during your stay:

The primary emergency number in Bonaire is 911. This number connects you to emergency services, including police, fire, and medical assistance. You can dial 911 from any phone, and operators will assist you based on your emergency.

For police assistance in non-emergency situations, you can contact the Bonaire Police Department. Their main phone number is +599 715 8000. The police station is located in Kralendijk, the capital of Bonaire.

In case of a fire or other fire-related emergencies, you can contact the Bonaire Fire Department. Their emergency number is also 911. For non-emergency inquiries, you can reach them at +599 717 8200.

For urgent medical help, call 911. Bonaire has a main hospital, Fundashon Mariadal Hospital, which provides comprehensive medical services. The hospital is located in Kralendijk, and their phone number is +599 715 8900. They offer emergency medical care, general medical services, and specialist consultations.

In case you need an ambulance, calling 911 will connect you to emergency medical services, including ambulance dispatch. Ensure you provide clear information about your location and the nature of the emergency.

For non-emergency assistance or general information, you can contact the Bonaire Tourism Corporation. They provide information on local services, safety tips, and other helpful resources for tourists. Their phone number is +599 717 8322.

If you are a foreign traveler and need assistance from your country's consulate, it's important to know the contact details of your country's embassy or consulate in the region. For example, the nearest U.S. Consulate is located in Curaçao, and their phone number is +599 9 461 3066. Make sure to check the contact details of your respective consulate before traveling.

In case of poisoning or if you need urgent information about toxic substances, contact the Dutch Caribbean

Poison Control Center at +31 30 274 8888. They can provide immediate guidance and support over the phone.

Having these emergency contacts saved in your phone and written down in a safe place can provide peace of mind during your trip. In case of an emergency, stay calm, provide clear and concise information, and follow the instructions given by emergency personnel. Enjoy your stay in Bonaire knowing you are well-prepared for any unexpected situations.

Health and Safety Tips

Ensuring your health and safety while enjoying the beauty of Bonaire is essential for a pleasant and worry-free trip. Here are some important tips to keep in mind:

Stay Hydrated:
Bonaire's tropical climate can be hot and humid, so it's vital to drink plenty of water throughout the day. Always carry a refillable water bottle with you and take regular sips, especially if you're engaging in outdoor activities like hiking, snorkeling, or exploring the island. Dehydration can sneak up on you, so make hydration a priority to keep your energy levels up and avoid heat-related issues.

Protect Yourself from the Sun:
The Caribbean sun is strong, and sunburn can quickly ruin your vacation. Apply a high SPF sunscreen generously and frequently, particularly after swimming or sweating. Wearing a wide-brimmed hat, sunglasses, and light, long-sleeved clothing can provide extra protection. Don't forget to seek shade during the peak sun hours, usually between 10 AM and 4 PM, to minimize your exposure.

Use Insect Repellent:
While Bonaire is relatively free of many tropical diseases, it's still wise to protect yourself from mosquito bites. Use insect repellent containing DEET, especially in the early morning and late afternoon when mosquitoes are most active. Wearing long sleeves and pants in the evening can also help reduce the risk of bites.

Be Cautious with Marine Life:
Bonaire's waters are teeming with vibrant marine life, and while most encounters are harmless, it's important to be aware of your surroundings. Avoid touching or stepping on coral reefs to protect both yourself and the delicate ecosystems. Some marine creatures, like lionfish and fire coral, can cause painful stings. If you're snorkeling or diving, maintain a respectful distance from all marine animals.

Practice Safe Diving and Snorkeling:
If you plan to dive or snorkel, ensure you are familiar with safety protocols. Always dive with a buddy and never exceed your certification limits. Check your equipment before heading out and pay attention to local weather conditions. If you're new to diving, consider taking a guided tour with a certified instructor to ensure a safe and enjoyable experience.

Respect Local Laws and Customs:
Familiarize yourself with Bonaire's local laws and customs to avoid any unintended offenses. For example, it's illegal to take any marine life or coral from the island, and strict regulations protect Bonaire's natural resources. Respect the environment by disposing of trash properly and following guidelines in protected areas.

Prepare for Emergencies:
Know the location of the nearest medical facilities and have emergency contact numbers handy. Bonaire has a reliable healthcare system, but it's always best to be prepared. Travel insurance that covers medical emergencies is highly recommended, ensuring you have access to necessary care without unexpected costs.

Road Safety:
If you're renting a car or scooter, drive cautiously. Roads in Bonaire can be narrow, and some areas are unpaved. Always wear your seatbelt and helmet if you're on a scooter. Be mindful of local wildlife, such as donkeys and iguanas, which may wander onto the roads.

By following these health and safety tips, you can fully enjoy the natural beauty and adventure that Bonaire has to offer while keeping yourself and your companions safe. Stay mindful of your surroundings, respect local guidelines, and you're sure to have an unforgettable and worry-free experience on this Caribbean gem.

Useful Apps, Websites and Map for Your Bonaire Trip

Exploring Bonaire is made easier with a selection of valuable apps, maps, and websites designed to enhance your travel experience:

1. Bonaire Insider: (www.bonaireinsider.com)
Dive into insider tips and local insights on Bonaire Insider. This blog keeps you updated on the latest events, hidden gems, and recommended activities across the island.

2. Bonaire Offline Map & Guide (App):
Navigate Bonaire effortlessly with this offline map and travel guide app. It provides detailed maps, dining options, accommodations, and essential travel tips, ensuring you can explore the island without needing an internet connection.

3. Windfinder (App):
Ideal for wind sports enthusiasts, Windfinder offers real-time wind and weather forecasts tailored for Bonaire. Whether you're into windsurfing or kitesurfing, this app helps you plan your outdoor adventures with precision.

4. Google Maps:
Google Maps is your go-to for navigating Bonaire's roads and discovering local attractions, restaurants, and places to stay. Its offline maps feature lets you save maps beforehand for uninterrupted navigation.

5. Bonaire Tourism Website: (www.tourismbonaire.com)
Visit the official Bonaire Tourism website for comprehensive information on attractions, activities, accommodations, dining spots, and upcoming events. It's an invaluable tool for crafting your itinerary and discovering the island's diverse offerings.

6. Bonaire Marine Park Website: (www.bmp.org)
Explore Bonaire's rich marine life and conservation efforts through the Bonaire National Marine Park website. This site details top dive and snorkel sites, conservation initiatives, and guidelines for responsible marine tourism.

These resources can help to enrich your Bonaire adventure, offering everything from insider tips to real-time weather updates and comprehensive travel information.

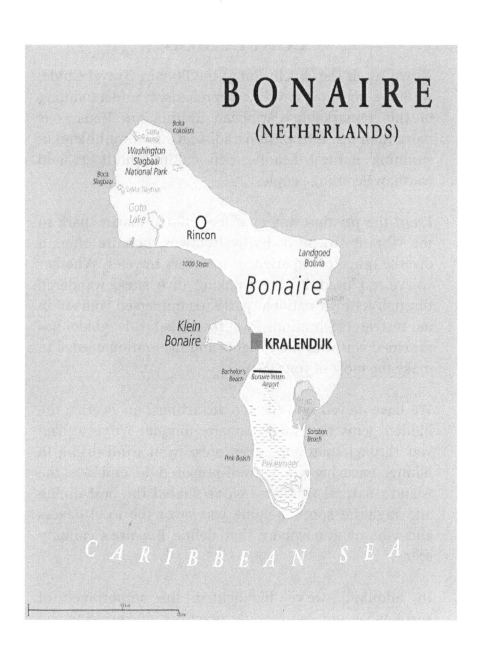

BONAIRE
(NETHERLANDS)

Boka Kokolishi
Suru Banda
Washington Slagbaai National Park
Boca Slagbaai
Salina Slagbaai
Goto Lake

O
Rincon

Landgoed Bolivia

Bonaire

1000 Steps

Klein Bonaire

KRALENDIJK

Bachelor's Beach
Bonaire Intern Airport

Sorobon Beach

Pink Beach
Pekelmeer

C A R I B B E A N   S E A

143

CONCLUSION

As we reach the conclusion of the Bonaire Travel Guide, we hope you now have a comprehensive understanding of this remarkable Caribbean destination. Bonaire is more than just a tropical paradise; it's a vibrant blend of stunning natural beauty, rich cultural heritage, and warm, welcoming people.

From the pristine waters of its national marine park to the vibrant streets of its lively towns, Bonaire offers a diverse range of experiences for every traveler. Whether you've explored its breathtaking dive sites, wandered through its lush national parks, or immersed yourself in its festive celebrations, we trust that this guide has provided you with the insights and inspiration needed to make the most of your visit.

We have delved into the top attractions, uncovering the hidden gems that make Bonaire unique. We've walked you through outdoor adventures, from windsurfing to hiking, ensuring you're well-prepared to embrace the island's natural wonders. We've shared the best dining and nightlife spots, helping you savor the local flavors and vibrant atmosphere that define Bonaire's culinary scene.

In addition, we've highlighted the importance of sustainable and eco-friendly practices, encouraging you to explore Bonaire responsibly. By supporting local communities and engaging in conservation efforts, you contribute to preserving the island's beauty for future generations.

Practical information on currency, language and emergency contacts has been provided to ensure your stay is smooth and hassle-free. With essential resources and tips at your fingertips, you can navigate Bonaire with confidence and ease.

As you reflect on your journey through this guide, remember that Bonaire is a destination that thrives on discovery. Each visit offers new opportunities to uncover its secrets and deepen your connection to this enchanting island. Whether you're a first-time visitor or a returning traveler, Bonaire promises unforgettable experiences that will stay with you long after you leave.

Thank you for choosing the Bonaire Travel Guide as your companion on this adventure. We hope it has been a valuable resource, enhancing your understanding and appreciation of Bonaire. May your travels be filled with joy, wonder, and lasting memories. Safe travels and happy exploring!

Made in the USA
Las Vegas, NV
27 December 2024

15429601R00085